STUDIES IN SOCIOLOGY

This series, prepared under the auspices of the British Sociological Association, is designed to provide short but comprehensive and scholarly treatments of key problem-areas in sociology. The books do not offer summary accounts of the current state of research in various fields, but seek rather to analyse matters which are the subject of controversy or debate. The series is designed to cover a broad range of topics, falling into three categories: (1) abstract problems of social theory and social philosophy; (2) interpretative questions posed by the writings of leading social theorists; (3) issues in empirical sociology. In addition, the series will carry translations of important writings in sociology which have not previously been available in English. Each book makes a substantive contribution to its particular topic, while at the same time giving the reader an indication of the main problems at issue; each carries an annotated bibliography, comprising a critical survey of relevant further literature.

ANTHONY GIDDENS

University of Cambridge

STUDIES IN SOCIOLOGY

General Editor: ANTHONY GIDDENS

Editorial Advisers: T. B. BOTTOMORE, DAVID LOCKWOOD and ERNEST GELLNER

Published

POLITICS AND SOCIOLOGY IN THE THOUGHT OF MAX WEBER
Anthony Giddens

PROFESSIONS AND POWER
Terence J. Johnson

THE SOCIAL PROCESS OF INNOVATION: A STUDY IN THE SOCIOLOGY OF SCIENCE
M. J. Mulkay

Forthcoming

THE SOCIOLOGY OF SOCIAL MOVEMENTS
J. Banks

MARXIST SOCIOLOGY
T. B. Bottomore

MATHEMATICS AND SOCIOLOGY
B. Hindess

STRIKES AND INDUSTRIAL CONFLICT
G. Ingham

THE DEVELOPMENT OF THE SOCIOLOGY OF KNOWLEDGE
S. Lukes

CONSCIOUSNESS AND ACTION IN THE WESTERN WORKING CLASS
M. Mann

MICHELS AND THE CRITIQUE OF SOCIAL DEMOCRACY
F. Parkin

Professions and Power

TERENCE J. JOHNSON
Research Fellow, Institute of Commonwealth Studies
University of London

Macmillan

First published 1972 by
THE MACMILLAN PRESS LTD
London and Basingstoke
Associated companies in New York Toronto
Dublin Melbourne Johannesburg and Madras

SBN 333 13430 3

Printed in Great Britain by
THE ANCHOR PRESS LTD
Tiptree, Essex

CONTENTS

ACKNOWLEDGEMENTS

Many of the ideas contained in this booklet are a by-product of a comparative study of professions in Commonwealth countries which was carried out at the Institute of Commonwealth Studies, University of London, and financed by a generous grant from the Social Science Research Council. I should like to thank Professor Morris-Jones and Michael Lee for reading an early draft of the manuscript and Georgie Wolton for casting a 'professional's' eye over the final product. Thanks are also due to Marjorie Caygill who read, re-read, researched and typed and generally tried to save me from gross errors of fact and judgement. Nevertheless, where they occur, the errors are all mine. In publishing this study I am also aware of an intellectual debt which is diffuse and difficult to assess but is the product of years of discussion with colleagues in the Sociology Department of Leicester University.

T. J. J.

1. THEORETICAL APPROACHES: CONCEPTS AND CONTRASTS

The increase in the number of professionals and the growth of professionalism has been generally accepted by social scientists as a major if not a defining characteristic of industrial societies. So much so that a recent president of the American Sociological Association felt able to assert as his first official utterance that 'An industrialising society *is* a professionalising society'.[1] Surprisingly, this general acceptance of the significance of professional occupations has not been fully reflected in theoretical analyses of the place of the professions in industrial and developing societies. While social commentators have been ever ready to identify the 'true' inheritors of power from among the ranks of the professionals – the 'technocrat', 'expert', 'organisation man', 'manager', have each in turn been seen as at least populating the corridors of power[2] – sociologists have, on the whole, tended to retreat in the face of these larger questions, digging in behind the defences of more circumspect analyses of a micro-sociological or social-psychological kind.[3] While the rapid growth of established professions and the emergence of new self-styled professional occupations have wrought significant changes in the class structures of industrialised societies, sociologists have focused attention on questions of attitude formation and socialisation into professional occupations.[4] While we have witnessed the rise of the professional

[1] W. J. Goode, 'Encroachment, Charlatanism, and the Emerging Profession: Psychology, Sociology and Medicine', *American Sociological Review*, xxv (1960) 902–13.

[2] The numerous attempts to identify emerging elites have, in general, been quite separate from the problems associated with the sociology of the professions.

[3] This point was made by Joseph Ben-David: 'The only more or less consistent trend (in the sociology of professions) has been an increasingly micro-sociological, or social-psychological approach to the problem.' See Ben-David (1963–4, p. 253).

[4] A recent evaluation of progress in this field is to be found in V. Oleson and E. W. Whittaker, 'Critical Notes on Sociological Studies of Professional Socialisation', in Jackson (1970, pp. 181–221).

bureaucracies such as the 'law factory' and the internationally-based accountancy firm, sociologists have turned to narrowly conceived problems exemplified by the numerous studies of 'role strain' in professional practice, examining the detailed consequences of conflicting expectations upon the practice of such occupations as social work, nursing, pharmacy, etc.[1] As a result the problems and themes which informed the origins of the sociology of the professions are either ignored in recent work or remain implicit.

The sociology of the professions received much of its initial impetus from two fundamental questions. The first concerned the extent to which professional occupations could be regarded as a unique product of the division of labour in society. The second question posed the problem : do the professions perform a special role in industrial society, economic, political or social? The first question stimulated Marx to attempt to establish the secondary and derivative character of professional classes, particularly in terms of their negative contribution to surplus value.[2] While for Marx the professions raised fundamental issues about the relationship between social differentiation and class structure, more recent sociologists have to a large extent concentrated on general aspects of social mobility and forms of stratification to the exclusion of an analysis of the division of labour itself. As a result the interest in the professions as a 'special' product of social differentiation has also been lost. Rather, the problem has been transformed into a largely sterile attempt to define what the special 'attributes' of a profession are. These definitional exercises litter the field. Or again, the question of the uniqueness of professional occupations is safely buried as a basic assumption which justifies the very existence of the specialist field we call the 'sociology of the professions'. Attempts to treat the professions as unique are based on the assumption that there is some essential quality or qualities which mark off the professions from other occupations and provide a basis for a distinct body of theory and variant forms of analysis.

[1] A variety of examples are to be found in B. J. Biddle and E. J. Thomas (eds), *Role Theory: Concepts and Research* (New York, 1966).

[2] Karl Marx, *Theories of Surplus Value* (vol. IV of *Capital*), trans. Emile Burns (London, 1969) part I, chap. IV, 'Theories of Productive and Unproductive Labour', pp. 152–304.

The second question which focused on the special role or functions of the professions in industrial societies has been largely operationalised out of existence. As sociologists set about analysing the part which the professions play in the various spheres of social life – in the economy or political system, as innovators or experts – they have tended to narrow down the original problem in order to handle it or as a reflex to demands for answers to specific social problems. They have split up the large question into smaller and more manageable components, dealing with such fashionable questions of the time as : what are the consequences of the growth of bureaucratic scientific organisations for the 'creative' role of the professional scientist;[1] or, more pragmatically, can we expect the scientist-bureaucrat to deliver the goods? Or again, under what peculiar institutional conditions do professionals – and this is related mainly to the medical profession – develop their characteristic sets of attitudes?[2] For example, can doctors maintain a highly personalised professional–client relationship in an increasingly impersonalised context? Each of these examples includes many cases where social-psychological questions concerning the generation and change of professional attitudes have superseded the more general sociological problems. Interestingly, one area in which the fundamental question of the overall social role of the professional remains significant is in the case of the military, but even here the problem is focused not on the professional soldier in industrialised societies, but on the political role of the military in developing societies.[3] In general,

[1] See W. Kornhauser, *Scientists in Industry* (Berkeley, 1962); W. O. Hagstrom, *The Scientific Community* (New York, 1965); S. Marcson, *The Scientist in American Industry* (Princeton, 1960); B. G. Glaser, *Organisational Scientists: Their Professional Careers* (Indianapolis, 1963); S. Cotgrove and S. Box, *Science, Industry and Society: Studies in the Sociology of Science* (London, 1970); W. Hirsch, *Scientists in American Society* (New York, 1968).

[2] See R. K. Merton *et al.*, *The Student-Physician: Introductory Studies in the Sociology of Medical Education* (Cambridge, Mass., 1957), and H. Becker, B. Geer, E. C. Hughes and A. Strauss, *Boys in White: Student Culture in Medical School* (Chicago, 1961).

[3] See J. J. Johnson (ed.), *The Role of the Military in Underdeveloped Countries* (Princeton, 1962); H. Daalder, *The Role of the Military in Emerging Countries* (The Hague, 1962); and S. E. Finer, *The Man on Horseback: The Role of the Military in Politics* (London, 1962).

11

the end-product of these trends in the sociology of the professions has been a widening gap between research and the theoretical problems suggested by the phenomenal growth of the professions and the implications of this growth for the changing distribution of power in industrial societies.

The neglect of these large-scale problems by sociologists has been associated with their nervous withdrawal from a 'value-laden' controversy in which on the one hand the professions were seen as a positive force in social development, standing against the excesses of both *laissez-faire* individualism and state collectivism, and on the other as harmful monopolistic oligarchies whose rational control of technology would lead to some form of meritocracy. Émile Durkheim was an early contributor to the first theme,[1] claiming that professional organisations were a precondition of consensus in industrial societies, and that the break-up of the traditional moral order initiated by the fragmenting division of labour would be rectified only by the formation of moral communities based upon occupational membership. The professions, he believed, 'should become so many moral milieux',[2] with the function of bringing cohesion to a society 'lacking in stability, whose discipline it is easy to escape and whose existence is not always felt . . .'.[3] He saw the professions as distinct from 'a whole range of collective activity outside the sphere of morals . . . and almost entirely removed from the moderating effects of obligations'.[4] This was the milieu of industry and trade in which individuals, while connected by competition, shared no common life of which the corporate occupational body was an expression. In England, Tawney also looked for an enlargement of professionalism.[5] In the 'acquisitive society', he believed, community interest had been subverted by the primacy of individual self-interest, and professionalism was the major force capable of subjugating rampant individualism to the needs of the community in a truly 'functional society'.

While Durkheim viewed professional ethics as the fount of a new moral order, others have gone a step further by specifying the

[1] É. Durkheim, *Professional Ethics and Civic Morals* (London, 1957).
[2] Ibid., p. 29.
[3] Ibid., p. 8.
[4] Ibid., p. 10.
[5] R. H. Tawney, *The Acquisitive Society* (London, 1921).

content of professionally engendered morality. For example, it has been suggested that professions are to be distinguished from other occupations by their *altruism* which is expressed in the 'service' orientation of professional men. In rejecting Laski's view that the debilitating individualism fostered by the existing professional institutions could only be countered by the creation of 'a great corporation under government control', T. H. Marshall (1939) claimed that state control would threaten the very 'essence' of professionalism :

> It [individualism] may mean the belief that the individual is the true unit of service, because service depends on individual qualities and individual judgement supported by individual responsibility which cannot be shifted onto the shoulders of others. That, I believe, is the essence of professionalism and it is not concerned with self-interest, but with the welfare of the client. (1939, pp. 158–9)

The view that the professions are actuated by the common good was restated by Talcott Parsons (1954), who pointed out that while business and the professions shared much in common in industrial societies, the professions were still to be distinguished by their collectivity-orientation rather than self-orientation. For Parsons, such an orientation ensured that science would be applied in the service of man.

More recently, Paul Halmos (1970) has reintroduced a Durkheimian theme in claiming that the professional service ethic is in process of penetrating the ideologies of all groups and institutions in industrial society, including business. In Halmos's view, while the ethic of 'personal service' originates in those professions such as medicine and social work whose 'principal function is to bring about changes in the psycho-social personality of the client',[1] it has subsequently spread to influence the self-image of other professional bodies. The 'personal service professions' are, he claims, the leaders in the creation of a new moral uniformity, a moral order influencing all industrial societies, whatever their political structure.

Closely connected with the theme of professional altruism has

[1] P. Halmos, *The Personal Service Society*, Inaugural Lecture (University College, Cardiff, 1966) p. 5.

13

been the claim that the professions have functioned as a bulwark against threats to stable democratic processes. For example, in the 1930s Marshall argued that it was the role of the professions to 'find for the sick and suffering democracies a peaceful solution of their problems' (1939, p. 170). But perhaps the most sustained and eloquent expression of this theme is to be found in the work of Carr-Saunders and Wilson (1933), who saw the professions as among the most 'stable elements in society'. The professions, they claimed,

> inherit, preserve and pass on a tradition . . . they engender modes of life, habits of thought and standards of judgement which render them centres of resistance to crude forces which threaten steady and peaceful evolution. . . . The family, the church and the universities, certain associations of intellectuals, and above all the great professions, stand like rocks against which the waves raised by these forces beat in vain. (1933, p. 497)

A more recent commentator saw professionally induced stability as operating not only at a national but also at an international level :

> Our professional institutions are . . . an important stabilising factor in our whole society and through their international associations they provide an important channel of communications with the intellectual leaders of other countries, thereby helping to maintain world order.[1]

In the 1950s Lewis and Maude (1952) joined with Carr-Saunders and Wilson in identifying the great industrial and governmental bureaucracies as the major threat to the 'proper' functioning of the professions in Britain. Carr-Saunders and Wilson were the more optimistic, maintaining that the professions would remain the major social force freeing men from a slavish dependence upon the state behemoth. As an increasing proportion of the working population gained admission to the 'great' professions, a larger number would share the institutional base from

[1] K. Lynn, Introduction to 'The Professions', *Daedalus* (1963, p. 653).

which men can enjoy a measure of 'freedom, dignity and responsibility' (1933, p. 503).

The mention of bureaucracy introduces the second major
theme of this controversy and a more sceptical view of the role of
the professions in modern society. Among social scientists, the
economists have most consistently questioned the benefits of professionalism, pointing instead to the harmful monopolistic practices of professional associations.[1] For such critics, the professional
corporations are far from anti-bureaucratic; they themselves are
bureaucratic mechanisms with the function of enforcing monopolistic practices. Among the sociologists, Weber did not distinguish radically between the consequences of professionalisation
and bureaucratisation and specifically linked the process of
bureaucratisation with the development of specialised professional education. He saw both processes as expressions of the
increasing rationalisation of Western civilisation.[2] While Weber
would have agreed with Carr-Saunders and Wilson that the professions bring 'knowledge to the service of power', he saw this
convergence not as a limitation upon the exercise of power
through the humanising agency of the professions, but as one
element in the process of rationalisation. It was a process in which
the professional as technician or expert was caught up in the
bureaucratic machine, as one of its creatures.

Among the sociologists who argued that Weber's prophecies
of bureaucratic hegemony have been at least partially fulfilled
was C. Wright Mills, who feared that the professions were increasingly succumbing to a 'managerial demiurge':

. . . most professionals are now salaried employees; much pro-

[1] See Lees (1966), and S. Kuznets and M. Friedman, *Income from
Independent Practice* (National Bureau of Economic Research,
Washington, 1945).

[2] It is interesting for the subsequent argument that Parsons, who
presents a 'functionalist' view of the professions, criticises Weber for
'his failure to bring out the structural peculiarities of the modern
professions and to differentiate between the organisation of professional services and what may be called the "administrative hierarchy" of occupational structure types. His "bureaucracy" is a
composite of both.' See Parsons's introduction to Max Weber, *The
Theory of Social and Economic Organisation* (New York, 1964) p. 54.

fessional work has become divided and standardised and fitted into new hierarchical organisations of educated skill and service, intensive narrow specialisation has replaced self-cultivation and wide knowledge; assistants and sub-professionals perform routine, although often intricate tasks, while successful professional men become more and more the managerial type.[1]

The continued expansion of professional numbers and the professionalisation of occupations was seen by Wright Mills not as a desired expansion of the learned and liberal professions dedicated to service, stability and democracy, but as an explosion of experts and technocrats – men of narrow specialism and narrower vision.

It has also been argued that the fusion of knowledge and power has created a new kind of professional-technocrat who is in process of replacing existing ruling groups. The professional-technocrats, it is suggested, would form an elite on the basis of 'merit' and as a result of such legitimation would enjoy a more complete and more secure authority than any historical ruling class.[2] James Burnham located the dynamic of such a development in the 'managerial revolution', claiming that the revolution consisted of a 'drive for social dominance, for power and privilege, for the position of ruling class by the social group or class of managers'.[3]

In comparing these two major themes in the literature it is evident that while the first concentrates attention upon the organisation and practice of professions such as medicine, law, architecture, social work, etc., this second theme draws its main illustrations from the fields of science, engineering and other professions intimately involved in corporate situations and management structures. Veblen, in contributing to the second theme, goes so far as to name the professional engineer as the natural decision-maker in modern industrial society:

> It will be no longer practical to leave its [the industrial system] control in the hands of businessmen working at cross-purposes for private gain, or to entrust its continued administration to

[1] C. Wright Mills, *White Collar* (New York, 1956) p. 112.
[2] M. Young, *The Rise of the Meritocracy* (London, 1958).
[3] J. Burnham, *The Managerial Revolution* (Harmondsworth, 1945) p. 73.

less than suitably trained technological experts . . . the material welfare of the community is unreservedly bound up with the due working of this industrial system and therefore with its unreserved control by the engineers, who alone are competent to manage it.[1]

While Veblen unequivocally places the engineers at the head of the ranks of professional-technocrats, Merton singles them out as a profession imbued with a 'trained incapacity for thinking about and dealing with human affairs'.[2] According to Merton, not only are the engineers unfitted for the elite status wished upon them by Veblen, but they lack those very characteristics which have been widely regarded as the 'essence' of professionalism. Merton argues that the social perspective of the engineer derives from bureaucratic employment as well as a high level of functional specialisation within the profession. The result of specialisation is that engineers 'come to be indoctrinated with an ethical sense of limited responsibilities'.[3] While presenting opposing views of the engineer, both Veblen and Merton would appear to reject the view that professionalisation inexorably leads to an increasingly participatory democratic society.

The professions, then, have presented to the social scientist two profiles: Janus-headed, they promise both a structural basis for a free and independent citizenry in a world threatened by bureaucratic tyranny and at the same time themselves harbour a threat to freedom. On the one hand altruistic motivation and a collectivity-orientation have been imputed to the professional, on the other he is said to suffer from a trained incapacity for social responsibility. Such inconsistent views may be explained by the fact that they relate to different professions at different points in time and also that contradictory processes may exist in the development of any single profession. However, such an explanation would undermine the view that the professions are a homogeneous group of occupations sharing a unique character and destiny. The theoretical attempt to account for such diverse and

[1] T. Veblen, *Engineers and the Price System* (New York, 1921) p. 33.
[2] R. K. Merton, 'The Machine, the Worker and the Engineer', *Science*, cv (Jan 1947) 79–81.
[3] Ibid., p. 80.

inconsistent interpretations of professionalism has centred upon the concept of *professionalisation*. It is claimed that we must expect variation in the nature of professional practice, attitudes and organisation if only because not all those occupations scrutinised are equally professionalised. Certain occupations, such as social work, teaching and accountancy, are not highly advanced in the process of professionalisation, while others, such as law, medicine and architecture, are closer to the end-state of professionalism. Occupations which stand at the extreme poles of the process are, therefore, bound to exhibit real differences. In attempting to reconcile the inconsistent interpretations of the social role of the professions, the theory of professionalisation has excluded the one element which was constant in earlier approaches: the attempt to understand professional occupations in terms of their power relations in society – their sources of power and authority and the ways in which they use them.

2. PROFESSIONALISATION AND PROFESSIONALISM

The concepts of professionalisation and professionalism have provided sociologists with the means of encompassing variations and seeming inconsistencies in the development and present state of the occupations conventionally regarded as professions. If ordinary people regard an occupation as a profession, it is argued, then it follows that there must be some fundamental similarity in the nature of such occupations which sociological theory should encompass. The fact that there are manifest differences in the prestige attaching to law and teaching or medicine and social work presents a problem which the concept of professionalisation has been developed to resolve. The term 'professionalisation' is used in a variety of ways, however, and it would be useful to distinguish between some of these before looking at its uses in more detail.

First, it is used to refer to broad changes in the occupational structure whereby professional or even white-collar jobs increase in number relative to other occupations, whether as a result of the expansion of existing occupational groups such as electrical engineers, or as a result of the emergence of new service occupations such as computer programmers. While a number of conclusions have been drawn from this general process and the level of social mobility which it implies – arguments in the late 1950s in Britain about the consequences of this trend for the failure of the Labour Party are a case in point[1] – the theoretical underpinning in this area of analysis is minimal and the interpretation of trends highly speculative. Secondly, the term 'professionalisation' is used in a way which implies little more than an increase in the number of occupational associations attempting to regularise recruitment to and practice in a specific occupation.[2] This usage is related to a concentration on the functions of qualifying associations, such

[1] M. Abrams and R. Rose, *Must Labour Lose?* (Harmondsworth, 1960).
[2] The significance of the professional association in the process of professionalisation is discussed in detail in Millerson (1964).

associations being regarded as the major indicator of the degree of professionalisation of an occupation. A third usage views professionalisation as a much more complex process in which an occupation comes to exhibit a number of attributes which are 'essentially' professional and are said to be the core elements of professionalism.[1] The existence of a qualifying association is only one such attribute. Finally, professionalisation necessarily refers to a process and there is sometimes the explicit argument put forward that this process occurs as a determinate sequence of events; that in the process of professionalisation an occupation passes through predictable stages of organisational change, the end-state of which is professionalism.[2]

In the last two examples, then, professionalisation is viewed as a process with an end-state towards which certain occupations are moving and others have arrived. For example, Vollmer and Mills suggest 'that the concept of a profession be applied to an *abstract model* of occupational organisation, and that the concept of "professionalisation" be used to refer to the *dynamic process* whereby many occupations can be observed to change *certain crucial characteristics* in the direction of a profession' (1966, pp. 7–8). The definition of what a profession *is* becomes a matter of pinpointing what these 'crucial characteristics' are. Such models – more or less abstract – abound in the literature. Theoretical statements have been largely restricted to a discussion and exposition of these characteristics. The result has been a confusion so profound that there is even disagreement about the existence of the confusion. For example, Goode concludes from a review of the literature that 'If one extracts from the most commonly cited definitions all the items which characterise a profession . . . a commendable unanimity is disclosed; there are no contradictions and the only differences are those of omission'.[3] That this degree of self-satisfaction is not shared by all sociologists is indicated by Millerson, who asserts that 'Of the dozens of writers on this sub-

[1] Among the better-known attempts to specify these core elements are E. Greenwood, 'Attributes of a Profession', *Social Work*, II 3 (July 1957) 44–55, and M. L. Cogan, 'Toward a Definition of Profession', *Harvard Educational Review*, XXIII (1953) 33–50.

[2] This approach is to be found in Wilensky (1964, pp. 137–57), and T. Caplow, *The Sociology of Work* (New York, 1954) pp. 139–40.

[3] Goode, op. cit., p. 903.

ject few seem able to agree on the real determinants of professional status'.[1] We may temper this confusion a little by dividing the existing approaches into two broad types, namely 'trait' and 'functionalist' models of the professions. While in specific instances these two approaches merge one into the other, they will be treated as distinct for the purpose of discussion.

'Trait' models of professionalism tend to be less abstract in formulation and comprise a list of 'attributes' which are said to represent the common core of professional occupations. The second approach is more abstract and is marked by a greater degree of explanatory intent. In the formulation of 'functionalist' models there is no attempt to present an exhaustive list of 'traits'; rather the components of the model are limited to those elements which are said to have functional relevance for society as a whole or to the professional–client relationship.

An illustration of the 'trait' model approach is to be found in the work of Millerson, in which he lists, after a careful canvass of the sociological literature, twenty-three 'elements' which have been included in various definitions of 'profession' (1964, Table 1.1, p. 5). These twenty-three items are culled from the work of no less than twenty-one authors who have attempted variously to define or abstract the 'essential elements' of the 'true' profession. It is interesting to note from the table that Millerson presents that no single item is accepted by all the authors as essential to a profession and that in the case of nine of the 'elements' there is a sole advocate only. On the other hand, no two contributors are agreed that the same combination of 'elements' can be taken as defining a professional occupation. The table includes among the most frequently mentioned traits: (1) skill based on theoretical knowledge; (2) the provision of training and education; (3) testing the competence of members; (4) organisation; (5) adherence to a professional code of conduct; and (6) altruistic service.

The 'trait' approach has proved inadequate in a number of ways. First, such models implicitly accept as their starting-point that there are, or at least have been in the past, 'true' professions which exhibit to some degree all of the essential elements. The

[1] G. Millerson, 'Dilemmas of Professionalism', *New Society*, 4 June 1964, p. 15.

'ideal type', as it is sometimes referred to, is abstracted from the known characteristics of these existing occupations – medicine and law are taken as the 'classical' cases. On many occasions one is left with the overriding impression that the 'ideal' is in terms of what ought to be. This is very clear in the work of Lewis and Maude (1952) who, while stressing that independent practice is the essential element of professionalism, are clearly distressed by the loss of independence which professionals experienced in post-Second World War British society. It is also true that many of the analysts who have applied themselves to the task of defining what a profession is, are at times pleading a special cause relating to the claims of an occupational group which is currently striving for professional status.[1]

The procedure of listing attributes without any prior and explicit theoretical framework suffers a number of penalties. It is not uncommon, for example, to include within a list of 'essential attributes' categories which are not exclusive of one another; one factor is considered to be both an irreducible core element and yet is equally clearly in some way derivative of a second characteristic. Greenwood's[2] often-quoted attempt to mine the sociological literature in order to 'distil' such core elements suggests that systematic theory and professional authority are among the five necessary attributes of a profession, but it is also clear from his discussion that professional authority can be subsumed under the former category, as systematic theory is the source of professional competence and thereby professional authority over the client.[3] The important point here is that there is little attempt in the 'trait' approach adopted to articulate theoretically the relationships between the elements – whether there is a direct casual relationship between the growth of systematic theory and authority or whether such authority may have its source elsewhere. Also 'core elements' such as 'altruistic service' give rise to a problem of distinguishing between the levels of analysis used.

[1] Millerson (1964, p. 3) draws this conclusion from his survey of the literature: '. . . authors begin as historians, accountants, lawyers, engineers, philosophers, sociologists, etc. As a result group affiliations and roles determine the choice of items and bias. Usually the measures are presented with their own occupations in mind.'

[2] Greenwood, op. cit.

[3] Ibid., pp. 44–7.

While claiming, for example, that altruism is a characteristic of the occupational role, it is not always clear whether altruistic motivation is also imputed to the professional man. While the service ethic may be an important part of the ideology of many professional groups, it is not so clear that practitioners are necessarily so motivated.

Where no theoretical limitations are placed upon these model-building activities, it is in practice possible to include or exclude from the list any 'elements', such as those presented by Millerson, in a completely arbitrary manner. In practice, most authors are concerned to establish 'authority' for their lists by claiming consensus. 'Trait' theorists are in this respect among the more democratic members of the sociological community. The decision to include or exclude 'elements' appears also to depend on which occupations one wishes to endow with or deprive of professional status. The liberal or open-handed analyst will be the most parsimonious with his categories because the fewer essential elements he includes, the greater the number of occupations that can qualify. Concern for the fate of social work has led to greater abstraction and parsimony in the checklists.

'Trait' theory, because of its atheoretical character, too easily falls into the error of accepting the professionals' own definitions of themselves. There are many similarities between the 'core elements' as perceived by sociologists and the preambles to and contents of professional codes. Professional rhetoric relating to community service and altruism may be in many cases a significant factor in moulding the practices of individual professionals, but it also clearly functions as a legitimation of professional privilege. Unquestioningly to accept the professional code as a sociological law is, to say the least, premature, as it is to assume that the application of the codes is uniform in its beneficial consequences for different sections of the community. To take one example, the view that the profession of law mediates between the power of the state and the needs of the individual citizen is often expressed as a form of altruism whereby the lawyer is regarded as the guardian of the rule of law for the benefit of all. However, as Rueschemeyer (1964) has persuasively argued, the profession's vested interest in a given legal order renders its service irrelevant to those groups in the society who seek radical change in the existing order. The 'guardians' of all our liberties become, for the Black Power militant or the Women's Liberation adherent, the upholders of an exploitative system. It is also true that where services of the practising lawyer are very unequally distributed among class groups, the rhetoric takes on a hollow ring indeed. A correspondent of the London *Times*, commenting on the findings of the Monopolies Commission's *Report on Professional Services* (1970), was led to the conclusion that a number of the restrictive practices carried on by professional groups and justified on the basis of community welfare looked in fact 'rather [like] arrangements for making life easier for practitioners at the expense, one way or another, of their clients'.[1] It is interesting that such comments and the Report itself indicate greater public scepticism of professional claims than is evident in much of the sociological literature, deriving as it does so many of its categories from the professional rhetoric itself.

Not only do 'trait' approaches tend to incorporate the professionals' own definitions of themselves in seemingly neutral categories, but the categories tend to be derived from the analysis of a very few professional bodies and include features of professional organisation and practice which find full expression only in Anglo-American culture at a particular time in the historical development of these professions. Perhaps the clearest example of this emphasis is to be found in the work of Goode, who argued that there is a necessary relationship between the existence of a developed professional community based on shared identity, values, role definitions, etc., and the acceptance of professional authority by laymen (1957, pp. 194–200). The major point I would wish to make in relation to Goode's general argument is that each of the characteristics of 'professional community' mentioned can itself be seen to have been undergoing a process of erosion in a number of pprofessions and to have never developed to any great extent in others. His 'model' neglects entirely the recent history of the professions whereby technological change has produced conditions throwing up new occupations to challenge the hegemony of the old; where existing professions have been subject to continuous differentiation; where changing client demands have reinforced trends towards differentiation and new sources of external authority have arisen to challenge

---

[1] *The Times*, 29 Oct 1970.

that of the professional community.[1] Goode's picture is an ideal one, of course, but the question remains : are the structural characteristics of 'community' still (and have they ever been) the most significant elements of professional existence? A problem which confronts all attempts to establish 'traits' of professionalism which are of universal applicability is that few scholars have attempted to establish the space and time dimensions and limitations of the concepts which they use,[2] though few would, if pressed, deny that they might have limited historical applicability.

While professionalisation necessarily refers to a process, then, the 'trait' model adduced as a checklist for the measuring of the degree to which an occupation is professionalised is itself fundamentally ahistorical. While empirical departures from the 'trait' model are conceived of as departures from an ideal type, they may also be considered the result of pathological conditions which retard the full flowering of a profession. The application of such a model blinds us to the possibility that occupations may develop variant forms of organisation and exhibit radical differences of structure despite the fact that the name of the game remains as a historical survival. Such models impose upon us – as does the very concept of professionalisation – a unilineal view of the development of selected occupations. But perhaps most fundamental to the following argument is that these models are not definitions of occupations at all, but specify the characteristics of a peculiar institutionalised form of occupational control. This confusion between the essential characteristics of an occupation and the characteristics of a historically specific institutionalised form of its control is the most fundamental inadequacy of both 'trait' and 'functionalist' approaches to the study of the professions.

Two extensions of the 'trait' theory approach may be briefly mentioned here, as they attempt to go beyond mere catalogues of 'elements' or 'characteristics'. The first is the attempt to operationalise the 'attributes' which characterise the ideal-type pro-

[1] A discussion of the consequences of differentiation within professional occupations and a critique of Goode's 'community' concept is presented by Bucher and Strauss (1961).
[2] This point is made by G. Harries-Jenkins, 'Professionals in Organisations', in Jackson (1970, p. 67).

fession in order to provide a number of measurable indicators of the process of professionalisation. Hickson and Thomas[1] have attempted to establish a hierarchy of professions in Britain by feeding measurable indicators of 'professionalism' into a Guttman cumulative scale. The scale is based on the 'elements' shown in the Millerson table referred to on p. 23 above. Unfortunately, the authors are forced to eliminate from the scale those characteristics which feature most prominently in the discussions of 'elements' by 'trait' theorists; that is, the degree of autonomy enjoyed by the occupations, the extent to which practice is based upon theoretical knowledge, and the degree of observation of the ideal of altruistic service.[2] Even so, they appear happy that the professionalisation scores they achieve for forty-three qualifying associations have credence because they seem to be in accordance with what one would expect; the external criteria of 'credence' are not made at all clear. They also point out the fact that the scale produces a fairly close relationship between the professionalisation scale score and the age of the various associations included in their study (a correlation of 0·41). This leads them to suggest that professionalisation is 'a long-drawn-out process'.[3]

The last point brings us to a further extension of the 'trait' theory approach, which is that these indicators of professionalisation can also be said to reflect a determinate historical sequence of events through which all professionalising occupations pass in an identical series of stages. The 'natural history of professionalism', as it has been called, finds its major expression in the work of Caplow and Wilensky.[4] For Wilensky, the natural history of professionalism in the United States has consisted of five stages: (1) the emergence of a full-time occupation; (2) the establishment of a training school; (3) the founding of a professional association; (4) political agitation directed towards the protection of the association by law; and (5) the adoption of a formal code (1964, pp. 142–6). It is clear that the sequence out-

[1] D. J. Hickson and M. W. Thomas, 'Professionalisation in Britain: A Preliminary Measurement', *Sociology*, III (Jan 1969) 37–53.

[2] Ibid., Table 2, 'Professionalisation Items and Scale Values', pp. 41–2.

[3] Ibid., pp. 48–9.

[4] Caplow, *The Sociology of Work*, and Wilensky (1964).

lined here by Wilensky (and this is true of Caplow also[1]) is historically specific and culture-bound. A simple and instructive example of cultural variation is England where, in the case of the 'established professions' he refers to, there is a particularly clear variation in the sequence: generally speaking, the professional association has emerged before the founding of a training school, whether professionally run or university-based. It is possible to argue that this variation – and there are others – is associated with relatively weak professionalism in the United States, resulting from the attack upon all forms of monopolistic privilege which took place in the eighteenth and early nineteenth centuries.[2] This attack on privilege, leading in a number of cases to a state ban on professional monopoly, particularly in medicine, led to a variation in historical sequence and a relative shift in the balance of power towards academic institutions as against the professional bodies.[3] As a result, American professional bodies have been accrediting bodies rather than directly qualifying members through their own systems of training and examination as has been the case in England until recently. We may also doubt the existence of a 'natural history of professionalism' if we look at the case of the former British colonies where protective legislation was not always, or even generally, the result of professional agitation, but the result of government initiative. Neither did protective legislation necessarily follow from the founding of a professional association or the creation of training schools in each case, but often, by contrast, brought them into being. These variations in sequence and timing suggest that there is no uniform or unilineal process of professionalisation which is of universal applicability, and that variations in the role of governments and academic organisations will substantially affect the control and

[1] Caplow (ibid., pp. 139–40) outlines the sequence as: (1) the establishment of a professional association; (2) change in the name of the occupation; (3) development of a code of ethics; (4) prolonged political agitation to obtain the support of public power; (5) the concurrent development of training facilities.

[2] See the extended discussion of this point in D. Boorstin, 'The Colonial Experience', chap. 7 of *The Americans*, vol. i (Harmondsworth, 1965).

[3] See J. F. Kett, *The Formation of the American Medical Profession: The Role of Institutions, 1780–1860* (New Haven, 1968).

institutional forms associated with similar occupational activities. The 'trait' approach to theorising about professionalisation, despite attempts to suggest a process and a chronology, is then ahistorical to the extent that it ignores variations in the historical conditions under which variant institutionalised forms of occupational activities develop. 'Trait' theory rarely includes any systematic treatment of the general social conditions under which professionalisation takes place. We may conclude that one of the underlying assumptions of the approach is that it is the inherent qualities of an occupational activity which autonomously determine the way in which institutional forms of control will develop – neglecting any reference to the effects of such factors as the prior existence of powerful and entrenched occupational groups, or the extent to which governments or academic institutions may impose their own definitions on the organisation of the occupation and the content of practice. Neither is there any systematic discussion of the fact that variations in the character of an existing or potential clientele are crucial in affecting the forms of development which are possible. This latter problem is generally referred to only in the cases of 'semi-professions' such as teaching, where it is concluded that the low status of the child-as-client is a significant factor in determining the low prestige of the profession.[1] When the structural conditions for 'professionalisation' are discussed, they are often confused with the defining characteristics of professionalism. It has been claimed, for example, that the emergence of a qualifying association or some form of controlling body, with the power to exert sanctions over its membership, or the development of educational institutions capable of providing lengthy periods of training, are among the conditions necessary for the emergence of a profession. Yet at the same time these very factors are claimed to be among the defining characteristics of the professions, and are therefore both cause and effect of the developments.

A more important line of theorising and research concerned with the conditions for professionalisation argues that the most rewarding approach is an examination of the circumstances in which claims for professional status are made. In recent years

[1] See T. Legatt, 'Teaching as a Profession', in Jackson (1970, pp. 169–71).

there has been a rejection of straight 'trait' theory and definitional exercises as fruitless and misguided activities which has been very much influenced by the work of Everett Hughes and his confession that 'in my own studies I passed from the false question "Is this occupation a profession?" to the more fundamental one, "What are the circumstances in which people in an occupation attempt to turn it into a profession, and themselves into professional people?" '[1] A similar argument was used more recently by Michael King, when he suggested that

> This line of approach avoids many of the pitfalls opened up by frankly evaluative definitions of the professions. It concentrates upon determining circumstances under which occupational groups make an avowal of professionalism and leaves to others the task of judging how close they come to living up to professional ideals. (1968, p. 40)

While it is true that many of the pitfalls of 'trait' theory discussed above might be avoided by this approach, it does raise similar problems in so far as it is wedded to the concept of professionalisation. By concentrating attention upon the circumstances in which claims for professional status are made, it is argued, we avoid the sterility of definition-mongering and instead focus on two of the major empirical phenomena of our times: group mobility through occupational upgrading, and the expansion of professionalism as a result of the growth of occupational group-consciousness. However, when either of these processes is identified with professionalisation it remains incumbent upon the analyst to state unequivocally what the nature of the process is and to have some idea of its end-state. In short, the claims for this approach are vacuous unless we are clear what a 'claim' for professional status entails. What is being claimed? What are the claimants aiming for? What are the consequences of such claims and under what conditions are they likely to be successful? All too often this form of analysis is taken as a short-cut to an explanation of professionalisation. That is to say, it is assumed that the claims for professional status are themselves *the* major conditions for professionalisation. What sources of power are available to an

[1] Quoted in Vollmer and Mills (1966, p. v).

31

occupational group making such claims is a question of crucial significance which is again often ignored. Also, as Prandy has pointed out, pressure by an occupational group to 'improve' itself may be class- rather than status-oriented.[1] Prandy suggests that engineering associations may be contrasted in that a number are geared to a direct attack upon the problem of increasing incomes while others are concerned with status inflation. However, even where the class orientation is basic to the aims of an occupational group, the ideological weapons of professionalism may be of great value in justifying their cause. For example, teachers will argue that their militancy in pursuing pay claims in recent years is fundamentally aimed at attracting a better recruit and thereby increasing professional competence and integrity.

It is not at all clear then that professionalisation refers to the same process as occurs when claims for professional status are made. However, professionalism is a successful ideology and as such has entered the political vocabulary of a wide range of occupational groups who compete for status and income – the latter has become much more manifest a process under various forms of income policy. As a result, the social functions of the ideology and the attraction of the 'professional model' for emergent occupational groups is a significant empirical problem and is worthy of attention. What must be borne in mind is that the ideology is espoused, either wholly or piecemeal, by occupational groups who have not achieved and are unlikely to achieve control over their own occupational activities. This is not because, as frustrated social workers are sometimes convinced, the leadership pursues misguided tactics, but because there exist external conditions which are antithetical to the development of the form of institutionalised control under which the occupation is paramount and autonomous.

The second theoretical approach to the sociology of professions distinguished above was that of the functionalist school. While much of the discussion of 'trait' theory could also be applied to

[1] K. Prandy, *Professional Employees: A Study of Scientists and Engineers* (London, 1965) pp. 30–47. Prandy distinguishes between class bodies which bargain with employers over pay and conditions and status bodies which seek to bestow and enhance prestige.

specific examples of functionalist theory, the argument will be limited to a discussion of those aspects of the theory which are peculiar to it. The components of functionalist models are limited to those elements which are said to have functional relevance either for the society as a whole or for the professional–client relationship.

Among the influential proponents of the approach are Bernard Barber and Talcott Parsons. The abstraction and relative parsimony of the functionalist approach are well illustrated by Barber, who claims that 'A sociological definition of the professions should limit itself, so far as possible, to the *differentia specifica* of professional behaviour'.[1] As a result, he excludes from his analysis such concepts as style of life, corporate solidarity and socialisation structures and processes which, he argues, apply to all occupational groups. Rather, he claims, professional behaviour may be defined in terms of 'four essential attributes' : (1) a high degree of generalised and systematic knowledge; (2) primary orientation to the community interest rather than to individual self-interest; (3) a high degree of self-control of behaviour through codes of ethics internalised in the process of work socialisation and through voluntary associations organised and operated by the work specialists themselves; and (4) a system of rewards (monetary and honorary) that is primarily a set of symbols of work achievement and thus ends in themselves, not means to some end of individual self-interest.[2] So far there is little to distinguish Barber's approach from those referred to above under 'trait' theory. However, in the succeeding analysis the functionalist orientation becomes clear. First, the significance of 'a high degree of generalised and systematic knowledge' stems from the fact that knowledge provides a 'powerful control over nature and society, [and as such] it is important to society that such knowledge be used primarily in the community interest'.[3] In Barber's analysis it follows that the repositories of such knowledge will exhibit a community rather than an individual interest, and as only the practitioners fully understand the implications of their own practices,

[1] B. Barber, 'Some Problems in the Sociology of the Professions', *Daedalus* (1963, p. 671).
[2] Ibid., p. 672.
[3] Ibid.

it is natural that they should be allowed the dominant role in controlling its application. While state power may play some part in controlling occupational activities, it will always be subsidiary to professional authority in the field of practice. 'Society', likewise, rewards practitioners in the form of money and honour as an appropriate means of rewarding such highly valued occupational performance. Honour tends to be more significant to professional practitioners because it is associated with the primacy of community as against individual interest. Businessmen, being self-centred, make do with money.

Ignoring the tautologies which are generated by such an argument, there are various criticisms which need to be levelled at the functionalist theory. It is possible to rest, in part, on the critique by Rueschemeyer, who claims that the functionalist approach can be basically characterised as positing that the professions are service- or community-oriented occupations applying a systematic body of knowledge to problems which are highly relevant to central values of the society (1964, p. 17). First, there is the assumption of functional unity which is clearly illustrated by Barber's position. It is assumed not only that the 'generalised and systematic knowledge' applied is of equal value to all groups in society, but that 'society' will react to ensure that those distributing the value will be mysteriously imbued with community interest and will be highly rewarded, again by 'society', as a means of sustaining such altruism. Rueschemeyer rejects the universality of such assumptions; in particular he questions that the 'central values' alluded to are shared equally by all sections and interests in society and that there will be an automatic feedback of status and autonomy to the profession as a result. He points out, for example, that law is not a scientific body of knowledge but a normative system and that as a result there are variations even in the conceptions of justice held by different socio-economic groups in a society. The law profession will not embody or apply values which are of equal relevance to all, and the values and organisation of that profession will vary in their consequences for different class or status groups. Rueschemeyer also attacks the implied view that a profession's status is related to the degree of complexity of the knowledge applied. He takes law as the example once again, pointing out that the lawyer to a large extent engages in activities which are central to the role yet do not depend on a systematic body

34

of knowledge but upon generalised interpersonal skills. It is also recognised that in the medical profession the general practitioner's skills are not even predominantly those of a skilled technician, but refer to the ability of the practitioner to relate in a warm and personal way to the patient who is seeking reassurance and a listening ear at least as much as a specific diagnosis and adequate treatment. It follows that the social distance which is generated in the relationship between the practitioner and the client is partly the product of factors other than the expertise of one and the ignorance of the other.

Parsons also points to the significance of central values in the emergence of professional occupations,[1] but by this he means not only the value of the content of a particular service, but the degree to which the professions in industrialised societies are the embodiment of what he calls the 'primacy of cognitive rationality' – that the professions represent a 'sector of the cultural system where the primacy of the values of cognitive rationality is presumed'.[2] In stressing the primacy of cognitive rationality and thereby the intimate relationship of the professions with the institution of science, Parsons overemphasises the degree to which rationality dominates not only the content of professional practice but also colleague and client relationships. The approach effectively eliminates from consideration the consequences of power relations within a profession whereby cliques representing specialisms or wider socially defined interests such as ethnic minorities may impose upon the profession role-definitions which are geared to maintaining their own dominant position at the expense of increasing the rational application of knowledge.[3] The emergence of a succession of subordinate 'professions auxiliary to medicine' in Britain is the history of how physicians have been able to define the scope of new specialised medical roles, and cannot be regarded as a hierarchy of semi-professions based upon the inherent potentialities for professionalisation of

[1] T. Parsons, 'Professions', in *The International Encyclopaedia of the Social Sciences* (New York, 1968) pp. 536–46.

[2] Ibid., p. 539.

[3] An examination of this thesis is to be found in H. Jamous and B. Peloille, 'Professions or Self-Perpetuating Systems? Changes in the French University Hospital System', in Jackson (1970, pp. 109–52).

each occupation, or even a product of the most rational utilisation of human resources.

In his analysis of the medical profession,[1] Parsons traces the primacy of cognitive rationality as it is expressed through such mechanisms as the 'functional specificity' and 'affective neutrality' of the professional role. That is to say that the doctor emphasises the technical bases of his role in his relationships with his patients and colleagues to the exclusion of external and non-technical considerations; such mechanisms function to sustain relationships of potential tension. While we can accept that the problem of tension management exists, Parsons's analysis again diverts attention from the consequences for the professional–client relationship of other significant social relationships. For example, it neglects the systemic importance of the social selection of patients and differences in modes of treatment which have been empirically shown to vary along class lines.[2] It also ignores the fact that affective neutrality and professional authority – the latter stemming from professional competence – are likely to operate only where they do not conflict with other and more important aspects of the relationship between professional and client. Where, for example, a physician or architect is subject to the whims of a single powerful patron as the sole client; where the client has the power to define his own needs and the manner in which they are to be met; then the relationships of affective neutrality and authority which Parsons claims are inherent in the professional role will be undermined. The professional–patron relationship is not merely an example of 'deviance' from the normal professional–client relationship, as Parsons would appear to suggest, but reflects an institutionally variant form of the control of occupational activities.

A deficiency in Rueschemeyer's critique of functionalism as applied to the sociology of professions is that he fails to consider the consequences of the ahistorical assumptions which are built into the approach as a result of which the functionalists can conceive of no alternatives to the form of institutionalised control

[1] T. Parsons, *The Social System* (New York, 1951) chap. x.
[2] See, for example, J. K. Myers and L. Schaffer, 'Social Stratification and Psychiatric Practice: A study of an Out-patient Clinic', *American Sociological Review*, xix (1954).

which they refer to as 'professionalism'. The argument here is essentially similar to that which has been directed against the functional theory of stratification. A functionalist analysis of stratification claims that existing differentials in social rewards are functionally related to the hierarchy of talent and ensure that such talent is made available for the fulfilling of 'society's' needs and the solution of 'society's' problems.[1] The critique argues that such an analysis is a distortion of reality because it neglects a historical explanation which indicates that any given reward structure is the result of arrogation by groups with the power to secure their claims and create their own system of legitimation.[2] In the same way, institutionalised forms of control of occupations are only to be fully understood historically through an analysis of the power of specific groups to control occupational activities. To achieve this understanding, we must make a clear distinction between the characteristics of an occupational activity (which may themselves change over time) and historically variant forms of the institutional control of such activities which are a product of definite social conditions. By introducing the time dimension, we can show that the changing distribution of power in society has had important consequences for the manner in which the producers of goods and services have related to their customers and clients.

So far, then, we have concluded that the concept of professionalisation and its end-state, professionalism, are based upon models which are an abstraction from the core 'elements' which are most fully exhibited by the 'true' professions. This approach has been supplemented in the literature by a functionalist model which stresses the functional value of professional activity for all groups and classes in society and in so doing excludes from consideration the power dimension, which in turn suggests possible variations in the institutionalised forms of the control of occupational activities. Neither approach is likely to provide the means of analysing real variations in the organisation of occupations in culturally and historically distinct societies. The concept of pro-

[1] See K. Davis and W. Moore, 'Some Principles of Stratification', *American Sociological Review*, v 10 (1945) 242–9.

[2] See M. M. Tumin, 'Some Principles of Stratification: A Critical Analysis', *American Sociological Review*, XVIII (1953) 387–94.

fessionalisation itself is a strait-jacket imposing a view of occupational development which is uniform between cultures and unilineal in character. As a concept it does not provide the means by which we might identify the structural bases for variations in occupational control, except in so far as they are deviant from the expected progression towards professionalism. Finally, a major weakness of attempts to develop theoretical statements about professional occupations has been the confusion which exists over what the object of study actually is – an occupational activity or the institutionalised form of the control of such activity. In accepting the professions' own definitions of themselves, sociologists have tended to accept that a peculiar institutionalised form of control is the *essential* condition of such occupations rather than being a peculiar historical product which can be said to have existed for a very short period and was a product of the specific historical conditions of nineteenth-century Anglo-American culture. It is necessary, therefore, to elaborate the theoretical framework of the sociology of professions in order to identify and account for these types of institutionalised forms of control. In seeking variations in the ways in which professional occupations have been controlled, we may eradicate the limitations inherent in the view that all such occupations may be placed upon a single continuum and are developing towards a uniform end-state. Also, by focusing attention upon the practitioner–client relationship, we must look to changes in the distribution of power in society as a major factor transforming the nature of the clientele and, therefore, the institutions of control.

3. TYPES OF OCCUPATIONAL CONTROL

Attempts to develop the concepts of professionalisation and professionalism in order to account for observed differences between occupations which are conventionally regarded as professions have concentrated attention on the institutional orders which have grown up around occupational activities. In general, they have ignored the prior problem of distinguishing between occupational activities as such. In identifying the nature of occupational activities we must first look at the general consequences of the social division of labour. In all differentiated societies, the emergence of specialised occupational skills, whether productive of goods or services, creates relationships of *social and economic dependence* and, paradoxically, relationships of *social distance*. Dependence upon the skills of others has the effect of reducing the common area of shared experience and knowledge and increases social distance; for the inescapable consequence of specialisation in the production of goods and services is *un*specialisation in consumption. This consequence flows from the crystallisation and development of all specialised occupations. While specialisation creates systematic relationships of interdependence, it also introduces potentialities for autonomy. It is social distance as a product of the division of labour which creates this potentiality for autonomy, but it is not to be identified with it. Rather, social distance creates a structure of uncertainty, or what has been referred to as indeterminacy,[1] in the relationship between producer and consumer, so creating a tension in the relationship which must be resolved. There is an *irreducible but variable* minimum of uncertainty in any consumer–producer relationship, and, depending on the degree of this indeterminacy and the social structural context, various institutions will arise to reduce the uncertainty. Power relationships will determine whether uncertainty is reduced at the expense of producer or consumer.

The fact that the level of indeterminacy is variable has important consequences for the relative autonomy of various occupa-

[1] This term is used by Jamous and Peloille in Jackson (1970). See the discussion on pp. 111–20.

tions and the resources available to one occupation as against another in imposing their own definitions of the producer–consumer relationship. The resources of power available to any single occupational group are rarely sufficient to impose on all consumers its own definitions of the content of production and its ends, except where these resources are articulated with other and wider bases of social power. The major exception to this rule is the modern professional army, whose technological and organisational resources are often sufficient to achieve this. A significant element in producing variations in the degree of uncertainty and, therefore, the potentialities for autonomy is the esoteric character of the knowledge applied by the specialist. However, this is not to follow the usual stress in the literature upon systematic theory as a basis for professionalism and professional authority. First, the term 'esoteric' is used advisedly, as it refers neither to the degree of the complexity of knowledge nor to the level of specialisation involved in an occupational activity. For example, while certain skills may increase in complexity, as measured by the level of training necessary for their application, it is not inconceivable that the general level of understanding of such skills could also increase with educational advance on a broad front. Social distance does not, therefore, automatically increase. Also, social distance is not in all circumstances a direct consequence of specialisation, as high levels of specialisation may expose an occupation to fragmentation and routinisation as a result of which it is more easily understood and controlled by non-practitioners. However, the technological conditions for routinisation within a given occupation will not necessarily lead to such fragmentation where, for example, the practitioners already control and define the content of practice. Accountants are already struggling against the consequences of routinisation heralded by the computerisation of a number of their activities, while printers are another well-known example of a group which has successfully retarded the introduction of technologies reducing the skill content of production.[1] The power relationship existing between practitioner and client may be such, then, as to enable the practitioner to increase the social distance and his own autonomy and control over practice

[1] See A. J. M. Sykes, 'Unity and Restrictive Practices in the British Printing Industry', *Sociological Review*, VIII (Dec 1960) 239–54.

by engaging in a process of 'mystification'. Uncertainty is not, therefore, entirely cognitive in origin but may be deliberately increased to serve manipulative or managerial ends.

The assertion made that an occupation group rarely enjoys the resources of power which would enable it to impose its own definitions of the producer–consumer relationship suggests that *professionalism* as defined in the literature is a peculiar phenomenon. It is only where an occupational group shares, by virtue of its membership of a dominant class or caste, wider resources of power that such an imposition is likely to be successfully achieved, and then only where the actual consumers or clients provide a relatively large, heterogeneous, fragmented source of demand. The polar opposite of this situation is where there is a single consumer – a patron who has the power to define his own needs and the manner in which he expects these to be catered for. In order to determine the variations which are possible in forms of institutionalised control of occupational activities, then, it is necessary to take account of the wider resources of power which are available to an occupational group and also to focus upon the producer–consumer relationship in so far as this is affected by the social composition and character of the source of demand.

While each of these factors will help to explain why certain institutional forms of control of an occupation arise, there remains the fact that occupational activities vary in the degree to which they give rise to a structure of uncertainty and in their potentialities for autonomy. It is this factor which provides an explanation of why it is that some occupations rather than others achieve self-regulation and even why they draw recruits from groups who already command alternative resources of power. Certain occupations are associated with particularly acute problems of uncertainty, where client or consumer judgement is particularly ineffective and the seeking of skilled help necessarily invites intrusion of others into intimate and vulnerable areas of the consumer's self- or group-identity. Medical practice, for example, intrudes into areas of social taboo relating to personal privacy and bodily functions, as well as areas of culturally defined ritual significance such as birth and death. In a similar way, the functions of a specialised priesthood may be regarded as fundamental to the well-being of a group. Such occupations involve social relationships of potential tension, where the provision of

43

specialised services is threatening and uncertainty compounded. The greater the social distance, the greater the 'helplessness' of the client, then the greater the exposure to possible exploitation and the need for social control. It is clear that a number of occupations conventionally regarded as professions are of this kind. Two points must be made here. First, while it is suggested that certain occupations are potentially threatening and exploitative, we do not need to conclude that this will be equally so for all groups in a society, nor that the service is equally valued. In short, the functionalist reification of a 'central societal value' must be avoided. As pointed out above, the values associated with law are not equally shared, and the apparatus of a legal order has functions for the maintenance and legitimation of a dominant group and explains why law should be regarded as a 'fit' occupation for members of or aspirants to an upper class.

Secondly, an occupation may undergo changes in its skill content and cultural significance over time. As a result its potentialities for autonomy will also vary. The decline in the significance of the priesthood in England is a case in point. The decline in its cultural significance during the twentieth century has led to a decline in status and income and a reduction in the number of recruits from upper-class backgrounds.[1] It is also true that in mass-consumption societies new occupations have emerged which give rise to acute problems of control as a result of their cultural significance in such societies. The servicing mechanics are a case in point – a series of occupations which give rise to new forms of exploitation and need for social control.

Historically, various social mechanisms have arisen to 'manage' these areas of social tension which present problems of social control. A characteristic form of traditional control is where the quality of a good or service is guaranteed by a blood relationship only. For example, with the rise of large-scale business houses in Renaissance Italy, the initial means of controlling the operations of a factor or agent in distant markets was to send a family member or to tie him to the family by marriage.[2] In more modern times, the contract, the free market, and even branded goods have

[1] See B. Wilson, *Religion in a Secular Society* (Harmondsworth, 1969).

[2] Max Weber, *A General Economic History*, trans. F. H. Knight (London, 1923).

44

all fulfilled similar functions. They are an expression of moral orders associated with the existing division of labour and they consist of rules and conventions about who can do what and to whom and when. They are aspects of institutionalised forms of control which vary not only in association with changes in the content of knowledge and skills associated with an occupation, but also in response to emerging social problems and needs which are to a large extent the product of changing power relations. Those occupations which are associated with peculiarly acute tensions, as described above, have given rise to a number of institutionalised forms of control, 'professionalism' being one. Professionalism, then, becomes redefined as a peculiar type of occupational control rather than an expression of the inherent nature of particular occupations. A profession is not, then, an occupation, but a means of controlling an occupation. Likewise, professionalisation is a historically specific process which some occupations have undergone at a particular time, rather than a process which certain occupations may always be expected to undergo because of their 'essential' qualities. In order to place this peculiar form of occupational control in context, a typology of institutionalised orders of control will be suggested and the various characteristics of each order and the conditions for their emergence discussed.

While the typology presented below is expected, in a more developed form, to apply to all occupations, for the purpose of the present argument the discussion will be restricted to those occupations conventionally regarded as professions. In drawing up a typology it has been found useful to focus on the core of uncertainty – the producer–consumer relationship. There are three broad resolutions of the tension existing in the producer–consumer relationship which are historically identifiable :

1. In which the producer defines the needs of the consumer and the manner in which these needs are catered for. This type will be referred to as *collegiate* control and is exemplified by the emergence of autonomous occupational associations. Identifiable sub-types of *collegiate* control are *professionalism*, which in its most fully developed form was the product of social conditions present in nineteenth-century Britain, and *guild* control which emerged as one of the phenomena associated with urbanisation

in late medieval Europe. The following discussion will be restricted to professionalism, which followed the rise to power of an urban middle class and attained its most extreme expression in the organisation of law practice in England.

2. In which the consumer defines his own needs and the manner in which they are to be met. This type includes both oligarchic and corporate forms of *patronage* as well as various forms of *communal* control. *Oligarchic patronage* has arisen in those traditional societies where an aristocratic patron or oligarchy was the major consumer of various types of services and goods – where the artist and craftsman, architect and physician, were tied to the great houses. *Corporate patronage* refers to the condition in which occupations such as accountancy find themselves in present-day industrialised societies, where a major part of the demand for their services comes from large corporate organisations. Communal control refers to a situation where a community as a whole or a community organisation imposes upon producers communal definitions of needs and practice. This has occurred in isolated pioneering communities, but finds more modern expression in the development of consumer politics, whereby consumer organisations deliberately set out to control the quality and eventually the organisation of the production of goods and services.

3. In which a third party mediates in the relationship between producer and consumer, defining both the needs and the manner in which the needs are met. There are various institutional forms of this *mediative* type also, perhaps the most conspicuous example being *capitalism*, in which the capitalist entrepreneur intervenes in the direct relationship between the producer and consumer in order to rationalise production and regulate markets. No less significant, however, is *state mediation*, which will be the example discussed below, in which a powerful centralised state intervenes in the relationship between producer and consumer, initially to define what the needs are, as with the growth in Britain of state welfare policies. A further historical example was the role of the medieval church in Europe in regulating the practice of a large range of occupations.

There are many more possible resolutions of the basic tension in the producer–consumer relationship. For example, the needs

46

may be defined by one party, while the manner in which the needs are catered for is controlled by another. Whereas it can be argued that the state defines who is to receive medical services in Britain today, by and large medical practitioners continue to determine the manner in which these needs are catered for. A 'nationalised' occupation would exist only where the state defined both 'needs' and 'manner'. In accepting that there are variations in the control of 'needs' on the one hand and 'manner' of production on the other, we can take into account relatively subtle differences in the organisation of occupations which have created some difficulties in the literature on the professions.

It must be kept in mind that the impact of a prevailing system of control upon individual occupations will vary as a result of the prior historical development of the occupation. For example, an occupation which emerged in nineteenth-century Britain may bring with it into the twentieth century many of the symbols and organisational characteristics of *professionalism* (used in the sense indicated above), even though *professionalism* may be in decline and new institutional forms of control emerging. However, where a given set of social conditions is influential in affecting the development of occupations, there will emerge dominant institutional forms of control which will in turn vary from occupation to occupation in accordance with the potentialities for autonomy which a developing occupation exhibits. In the following analysis of each of the types outlined there will be a discussion of such factors as the nature of the consumer, the producer–consumer relationship, the conditions and characteristics of recruitment, colleague relationships, knowledge and ideology.

4. COLLEGIATE: PROFESSIONALISM REVISITED

Professionalism arises where the tensions inherent in the producer–consumer relationship are controlled by means of an institutional framework based upon occupational authority. This form of control occurs only where certain conditions exist, giving rise to common characteristics in organisation and practice.

For example, only where there exists an effective demand for the occupational skills from a large and relatively heterogeneous consumer group can the institution of professionalism fully emerge. Consumers will normally have diverse interests; they are unorganised, dependent and exploitable. Dependence arises out of the creation of needs which may themselves be differentially distributed according to socio-economic status. In Britain, for example, the incidence of problems defined as legal is higher in the middle class than in the working class, and as compared with medical services the elasticity of demand for legal services is greater. The degree of exploitability of consumers will vary, however. For example, where there is an accepted obligation on the sick to seek expert medical advice, the authority of the doctor is relatively high as compared with other occupations whose products and services are not obligatory and backed up by social sanctions in the same way. Family expectations and legal requirements act as a direct pressure upon the sick to seek the help of a doctor. Sickness is only legitimated for many purposes when the sick person is issued with a doctor's certificate.

Where the consumers are a large and heterogeneous group, any attempt by the occupation to extend technically-based authority to a broad social control of practice is likely to be more successful than in contexts where there is a single client or a small group of powerful clients. The social extension of an occupation's authority may be gauged by the degree to which its collective pronouncements on a wide variety of issues – perhaps only tenuously related to the field of practice – are regarded as authoritative contributions. While the legal and medical associations have been listened to with respect in England on such diverse issues as the economy, juvenile delinquency, drug use and the organisation of social welfare, the collective voice of architecture is muted even in areas directly associated with building policy. This is not to say that certain individuals and groups are not influential.

The conditions for professionalism developed in Britain in the second half of the nineteenth century in association with the rise to power of an urban middle class, which provided an expanding market for various services based largely on individual needs, whether private or entrepreneurial. The Industrial Revolution opened the floodgates of professionalisation. Scientific and technological developments crystallised into new techniques, providing a basis for emergent occupations. Needs which had been restricted to the upper stratum of society filtered down and outwards so that medicine, law and architecture, for example, were no longer small, socially prescribed cliques, but large associations servicing competing status groups of near equals. The potentiality for the creation of colleague-controlled institutions of practice also relates to the practitioners' membership of, or association with, an existing or emergent powerful social grouping. The status of a number of occupations had already benefited from association with aristocratic patrons, so marking them as 'gentlemanly professions'. For example, Carr-Saunders quotes a defence of physicians in the first half of the nineteenth century as enjoying

the great advantages which result to society from there being an order of men within the profession who have had an education with members of other learned professions; from a certain class of the medical profession having been educated with the gentry of the country, and having thereby acquired a tone of feeling which is very beneficial to the profession as a whole.[1]

The emerging urban middle class of nineteenth-century Britain not only created an expanding demand for professional services, but also provided recruits for the growing ranks of professionals. Middle-class power provided the basis from which the expanding 'professions' created their own autonomous organisations.

Under professionalism, the producer–consumer relationship

[1] Quoted by Carr-Saunders and Wilson (1933) from *Report of the Select Committee on Medical Education* (1834) part II, p. 20.

will normally be a fiduciary, one-to-one relationship initiated by the client and terminated by the professional. Consumer choice, a major element in consumer control, is weakened under such conditions and made ineffective by virtue of the consumers' heterogeneity and individualisation. In the development of medicine in England and even more so in Australia in the late nineteenth and early twentieth centuries, private insurance schemes, particularly those run by working men's benefit clubs, modified this situation by introducing a strong element of consumer control. The clubs attempted to force doctors into contracts which increasingly limited their freedom of action. For a short period they were very successful in imposing their own terms on practitioners, so retarding 'professionalisation' until the 'battle of the clubs' was finally won by the medical associations.[1] Even prior to the creation of national health schemes, the private insurance organisations had successfully influenced the structure of demand for medical services and also attempted to control the activities of practitioners. The one-to-one relationship under professionalism refers to the fact that solo practice is the norm, although various forms of partnership are possible. The fee is the all-important mechanism of defining client needs, and the client's only appeal is to a body made up of the relevant practitioners.

Professionalism is associated with a homogeneous occupational community. Homogeneity of outlook and interest is associated with a relatively low degree of specialisation within the occupation and by recruitment from similar social backgrounds. Where the norm of 'general practice' has given way to the proliferation of highly specialised sub-groupings, the community identity of the occupation is threatened by divergent interests and 'missions'.[2] It is likely then that a fully developed system of professionalism can emerge only where specialisation is relatively low. However, the culturally divisive tendencies of specialisation may be contained within an occupation already characterised by professional institutions. For example, the medical associations in Britain and the United States have been partly success-

[1] A G. McGrath, 'A History of Medical Organisations in Australia', unpublished Ph.D. thesis (University of Sydney, 1971).

[2] For a discussion of the significance of 'community identity', see King (1968).

ful in containing the disruptive consequences of the increasing pace of specialisation by subordinating new specialisms to the control of the dominant clinician and general practice groups. However, specialisation may also occur along lines defined by status differences among the consumers. Where, for example, an elite in the profession is engaged in providing services for an elite of consumers, differentiation of interests and even organisations may occur within the occupation. A number of studies carried out in the United States, for example, have suggested that lawyers and doctors from a low-status ethnic minority are likely to provide services for members of their own ethnic groups.[1] Such specialisation constitutes a further disruptive factor threatening the 'community' aspect of professionalism.

The major collegiate functions of the occupational group are carried out by a practitioner association or guild which bestows status and identity and attempts to sustain uniform interests among the members and promote uniform policies by imposing a monopoly on practice in the field and regulating entry to it. It is important to point out that the mere existence of an association or union is not in itself an indication of professionalism. For example, registration of practitioners which entails a monopoly of practice may be in the hands of the occupation, such as is the case with lawyers in England, or admittance to practice in a particular field may be controlled by a government department, as is the case with the auditing of public companies. In the latter case bureaucratic control is a severe limitation upon the development of professionalism. In the case of professionalism the occupational association is the registering body, and it develops effective sanction mechanisms for controlling not only occupational behaviour but also non-occupational behaviour. As a result, occupational homogeneity is reflected in colleague demands that a defined 'standard of conduct' be observed in areas of social life not directly linked to the provision of the service. The association will also attempt to impose a uni-portal system of entry to the occupation in order to ensure that shared identity is reinforced by the creation of similar experiences of entry and socialisation. It is

[1] See J. A. Carlin, *Lawyers on Their Own* (New Brunswick, N.J., 1962); E. O. Smigel, *The Wall Street Lawyer* (New York, 1964); H. J. O'Gorman, *Lawyers and Matrimonial Cases* (New York, 1963).

important to note here that the development of educational institutions providing 'recognised' courses for entry to such occupations, far from being an indication of the process of professionalisation, as is often argued in relation to the growth of vocational university courses, may in fact be symptomatic of de-professionalisation, by imposing on an occupation a multi-portal system of entry.

Under professionalism, a continuous and terminal status is shared by all members. Equal status and the continuous occupational career are important mechanisms for maintaining a sense of identity, colleague-loyalty and shared values. Also, the myth of a community of equal competence is effective in generating public trust in a system in which members of the community judge the competence of one another. The fact that the consumer initiates the relationship with the solo practitioner is a pressure towards isolation from the occupational community which is counteracted by a contact-network or referral system. The referral system can also be operated by the occupation to ensure that those members who most clearly exhibit the desired attributes and values of the occupation are favoured in their career. This system of selection is described in detail by Oswald Hall in his analysis of medical careers in a Canadian town.[1] Occupational norms are inculcated during lengthy periods of training. The assimilating institutions are characterised by close supervision within an apprenticeship system and peer-solidarity through the creation of vocational schools which are directly or effectively controlled by practitioners. Associational forms of organisation, a developed network of communication and a high level of interaction through branches, discussion groups, journals, 'social occasions', etc., all help to maintain the subculture and *mores* of the occupation which may be partly shared with other occupations but will also include elements specific to the occupational group. Where professionalism has been adopted as an ideology by occupational groups which are not professionalised, this 'sharing' is very widespread. Ritualistic elements are significant; legends, symbols and stereotypes operate in the public sphere to formulate public attitudes to the profession. The legend of Florence Nightin-

[1] O. Hall, 'The Stages of a Medical Career', *American Journal of Sociology*, LIII (1948) 327-36.

gale is certainly effective in the public sphere, as is the stereotype of the selfless nurse and the symbol of the white cap, with its religious connotations. A highly developed community language or jargon performs the double function of maintaining internal homogeneity and increasing autonomy from outsiders, both competing specialists and laymen. This is a widespread phenomenon which sociologists, who are often criticised for jargon-mongering, recognise only too well. However, there are a number of such occupations which experience peculiar difficulties in maintaining an autonomous means of internal communication because their concepts quickly enter into public use and as a result are 'debased'.

Finally, community-generated role-definitions and standards are maintained by a code of ethics and autonomous disciplinary procedures. This elaborate and formalised system of norms regularises such behaviours as securing appointments, conducting referrals, handling consultations, acquiring and receiving clients, recompensing a sponsor and relating to peers, superiors and subordinates.

While it has been argued that the Parsonian reification of values must be avoided, it is the case that under professionalism occupational ideologies lay great stress on the essential worth of practice. Justice, health and technological progress are variously regarded as the central values of social existence by the practitioners of each associated expertise. The occupational community regards itself as the repository of specialised knowledge, guaranteeing, for example, the autonomy of law and progress in the application of medical science for the public good. Prestige within the occupation is dependent upon colleague evaluation and, as a result, technical competence is a significant criterion of individual worth. Also, innovations in the application of basic research are prestigeful where they do not threaten the existing power position of the occupation in the society or dominant groups within the occupation. Rapid advances in experimental medicine and law codification were associated with the emergence of professionalism in Britain in the nineteenth century, yet many innovators, particularly in medical science, were pilloried, ignored or excluded by those who resisted the application of new technologies and knowledge. In all service-related matters the occupational community is believed to be wiser than the layman. From such beliefs the occupational community derives an ethical sense of full responsibility. No group is more morally outraged when laymen put forward opinions on occupationally related matters. At the present time, public concern in such fields as abortion and drug use is felt as threatening and in some sense an affront to medical practitioners. Attempts to extend occupational authority to wider areas of social life are at times pursued with missionary zeal and take on broad political significance. This is particularly true of law, for example, where social dissensus over conceptions of justice attracts lawyers into the political arena.

Professionalism creates occupations with a high degree of self-consciousness, and 'complete identity' (King, 1968). The core meaning of life is central to the work situation, and occupational skills are regarded as non-transferable – the property of a specific community. Charlatanism and quackery are, in this sense, a creation of professionalism and not the cause of it. That is to say that periods in which it is claimed that charlatanism is rife and needs to be stamped out are just those periods when an occupation is attempting to establish or struggling to maintain a monopolistic position. Practice can be unqualified only where a monopoly of skill by one group exists.

We are, in part, engaged here in an analysis of professionalism as an ideology. Elements of the ideology are most forcibly and clearly expressed by those occupational groups 'making claims for professional status' and engaged in an ideological struggle. Such occupations lay great stress on the need for occupational and individual independence as a precondition of fulfilling obligations to consumers. Among a number of service occupations this claim is associated with the emphasis laid upon the diagnostic relationship. That is to say, it is only in an unfettered person-to-person relationship with the consumer that expert diagnosis can take place and be successfully followed through. The diagnostic relationship is used as a control mechanism both within an occupation and in relationships with other allied occupations, for whatever the problem (mechanical, physical, psychological or social), action (plans, therapy or policy) stems from the diagnosis and the diagnostician assumes an authoritative role. The diagnostic relationship is given pre-eminence by those practitioners who personally confront laymen as an essential part of their work task and consequently need to have their expertise taken for granted. While physicians and lawyers often find themselves in this situation, scientists rarely do. The direct pressure of consumer scepticism upon individual practitioners is professionally controlled where equal competence in diagnosis is legitimated, and where external evaluations of diagnosis are effectively eliminated. The threat experienced by the medical profession in relation to drug use in Britain, for example, was actualised by legislation which defined some doctors as more competent than others in distributing 'dangerous' drugs to addicts. It is through control of the diagnostic relationship that the physician has maintained his pre-eminence in medical services. In Britain auxiliary health professions are defined by statute as 'professions supplementary to medicine'. This phrase indicates that physiotherapists, occupational therapists, chiropodists, dietitians, remedial gymnasts, etc., may carry out treatment only in respect of prior diagnosis by a doctor. As a result, the physicians have retained a position of authority vis-à-vis the patient, whilst subordinating emergent health groups to their own control and direction. The exclusion of osteopaths from the recognised health services can be explained in terms of their rejection of the right of doctors to diagnose and suggest a line of treatment for which doctors are unqualified to pronounce. The proliferation of subordinate professional grades is, then, a possible consequence of specialisation where the generalists are sufficiently powerful to maintain control of the professional–client relationship. An appreciation of these power relations which exist between occupational groups would help to resolve some of the problems which sociologists have experienced in attempting to define the characteristics of a number of those groups which have been called the 'semi-professions' or 'quasi-', 'marginal' and 'limited' professions.[1]

The ideology of professionalism claims a direct relationship between length of training and status – that high economic and social rewards are justified by the length of training necessary to acquire certain skills. In fact, the highest status has generally been achieved by those occupations where the technical content of the role is relatively low. Those professions which are 'client-based'

[1] See the preface to Etzioni (1969) and W. I. Wardwell, 'Marginal and Quasi Practitioners', in H. E. Freeman *et al.*, *Handbook of Medical Sociology* (New York, 1963) pp. 213–39.

and diagnostically oriented provide services in which the element of non-technical interpersonal skills is most important. This is the case with the lawyer, who is constantly involved in client problems which do not demand a high level of expertise in law, but general personal skills in human relations. Also, in England, where the law profession is divided between solicitors and barristers, the barristers, who are the 'specialists', receive a less impressive professional training than do solicitors, who operate as generalists to a much greater extent. Whilst within any given occupation the level of rewards is not invariably related to length of training through specialisation, it is an important fact that occupational groups use this belief as a major lever in their struggles for status. Thus, where professionalism exists as a form of control characterising only certain occupations, professionalism as an ideology is not restricted to groups who have undergone professionalisation. The pervasiveness of the ideology is not indicative of the extent of professionalism.

No occupation which is characterised by professionalism as a form of control is static and unchanging. There are major tensions existing within such a system which are constantly threatening its stability. A major tension at the core of professionalism is the conflicting pressure stemming from the relationship between occupational authority on the one hand and consumer choice on the other. As argued above, the existence of a large, heterogeneous clientele, exercising effective demand, is a condition of professionalism. At the same time the vagaries of consumer choice always operate as a counterbalance to occupational control in so far as they introduce pressures towards diversity within the occupational community. This occurs through such mechanisms as channelling fees in the direction of some professionals rather than others. Part of the function of a ban on advertising by various occupations is an attempt to minimise such a threat to homogeneity by limiting the degree to which the wealthy and influential members of the occupational community can take advantage of their already favoured position. Also, practitioners less favoured by the fee system will be likely to form a pressure group within the occupation seeking some modification in the producer–consumer relationship. This was the case with medical men who favoured the intervention of the state in creating a National Health Service in Britain.

Where the heterogeneity of the consumers is most significantly expressed in class or ethnic divisions, a systematic pressure towards differentiation within the occupation exists. One of the consequences of such divisions may be to produce within the field of health separate and even competing organisations of health provision – a public hospital system for the less well off and a private system for the rich. These organisations compete for resources, and practitioners develop divergent interests in the struggle for resources. Also, where law practices offer their services exclusively to one ethnic or class group, there will arise competing conceptions of the role of law and conceptions of justice within the profession itself. The occupational fission which results from these conditions is a consequence of 'client' specialisation rather than deriving from specialist techniques which, as has already been argued, are themselves a source of diversity. The class basis of practice in psychotherapy, for example, is reflected in the maintenance of competing therapies. It has been argued that the therapies associated with psychiatry on the one hand and psychoanalysis on the other are a product of different organisational contexts of practice which are themselves based upon class divisions.[1] The psychiatrist is characteristically located in the large-scale mental hospital geared to the low-cost supervision of patients. The constraints of the situation – large wards, large case-loads, etc. – are consistent with a therapy which stresses the physical basis of mental illness and employs drug therapy as a practical solution to the problems of treatment. Psychoanalysts on the other hand are oriented to the needs of the single fee-paying patient, or at least small group therapy, and as a result stress the psycho-social bases of mental illness and therapies based upon intensive long-term personal analysis. In each of the illustrations given, 'client choice' and the pressures inherent in 'client' diversity operate to set up strains in the system of professionalism as such and may lead to modifications in the institution which eventually reduce and in the long run may eliminate the conditions of professionalism itself.

In outlining the form of institutionalised control referred to as professionalism, it has been necessary to reassert a number of the

[1] A. Strauss *et al.*, *Psychiatric Ideologies and Institutions* (New York, 1964).

characteristics of organisation and practice which have been previously applied to *professional occupations*. It is hoped, however, that the following discussion of variant forms of occupational control will emphasise how limited in scope are arguments which accept that professionalism is inherent in the very nature of a few select occupations in whatever historical and cultural contexts they operate. It will be seen that professionalism cannot be viewed as applying to all 'professional occupations', but must take its place as one type of occupational control within a framework which allows for a more realistic, comparative approach to the problem.

5. PATRONAGE

The strains which create instability in *professionalism* as a form of occupational control also suggest the possibility of new controlling institutions emerging as a result of consumer power, where such power acts as a systematic source of pressure upon practitioners. Various forms of consumer control occur, and their institutionalisation gives rise to forms of occupational organisation, practices and culture which differ from *professionalism*. Discussion will be restricted to two forms of control, oligarchic and corporate patronage, in so far as they affect occupations which otherwise have a high potentiality for autonomy.

Fully developed institutions of patronage arise where consumers have the capacity to define their own needs and the manner in which those needs are catered for. In such cases the members of occupations applying esoteric knowledge are themselves 'clients', having neither exclusive nor final responsibility for their services; ultimate authority in the assessment of process and product lies with the patron or patrons. Patronage arises where the dominant effective demand for occupational services comes from a small, powerful, unitary clientele. This can occur where an aristocratic elite, sharing common interests, monopolises services. Similarly, a patronage system can develop where a few large-scale corporations are the major consumers of 'expert' services. Where these conditions prevail, the technically-based authority of an occupation and autonomy deriving from social distance are both at a minimum. The patron is relatively independent and unexploitable by virtue of his wider social bases of power. Uncertainty is reduced where the patron is in a position to define his own needs.

Oligarchic patronage is characteristic of traditional aristocratic societies such as seventeenth- and eighteenth-century England and Renaissance Italy.[1] In both cases a variety of occupations were largely restricted to the service and subject to the control of a

[1] For a detailed study of architectural patronage in England, see F. Jenkins, *Architect and Patron* (Oxford, 1961).

landed aristocracy. Corporate patronage, on the other hand, has been associated with the growth of bureaucratic organisation in industrial societies, creating conditions in which the demand for many occupational services comes increasingly from a declining number of large-scale corporations, both private and public. The significance of oligarchic and corporate patrons for any occupation is determined by the degree to which practice is not occupationally defined, but is imposed by the needs and definitions of clients.

The general characteristics of accountancy, as it has developed since the late nineteenth century in Britain, have been such that the occupation has always been subject to a large measure of corporate control. The modern accountancy profession was largely brought into being by the demands of corporate business, first as a form of internal company control and then as a form of accounting to the risk-bearer by means of a public audit.[1] The functions of the accountant in providing the means of cost or management control were regarded as so crucial for the development of capitalist enterprise that Weber defined the capitalist business firm as an 'establishment which determines its income-yielding power by calculation according to the methods of modern book-keeping and the striking of a balance'.[2] Accounting as a form of protecting the risk-bearer arose in association with the public joint-stock company whereby 'independent' auditors or accountancy firms reported on the financial position of a company to stockholders and to the public rather than to management. Despite the fact that all the early accountancy associations regarded themselves as primarily associations for 'independent' public auditors or accountants, their membership always contained a large proportion of employed accountants, while many independent firms carrying out auditing services have become increasingly dependent upon a few large-scale consumers of their services.

Under patronage, recruitment is based on sponsorship. The

[1] Histories of the accountancy profession include R. Brown, *A History of Accounting and Accountants* (Edinburgh, 1905; reprinted 1968 by Frank Cass), and N. Stacey, *English Accountancy, 1800–1954* (London, 1954).

[2] Weber, *A General Economic History*, p. 275.

criteria for sponsorship are shared values and statuses; that is to say, the professional shares the values and to some extent the status of the patron. Technical competence is not the sole or even a major criterion of evaluation. Rather, the practitioner is expected to be socially acceptable. This means that a small, servicing elite of practitioners share to some degree the social origins and characteristics of those who use their services. The operation of a patronage system in seventeenth- and eighteenth-century England gave rise to the notion of a 'professional' gentleman who was expected to share the tastes and values of his patrons and be socially fitted to take part in the life of the great houses. The growth of corporate patronage has been associated with selection of recruits on the basis of personality testing in order to ensure that they are personally 'acceptable'. In traditional systems of patronage, entrance to 'accepted' and exclusive occupational organisations is severely limited, while a developed corporate system results in the hegemony within the occupational associations of practitioners working for the more powerful corporations, whether as employees or consultants. This prestige has not, however, been accorded to all employed accountants, many of whom have been subject to exclusion from the governing bodies of the major associations in Britain. It has been the men associated with the more powerful corporations who have wielded power within the associations. This differentiation within the associations has been associated with the development of an occupational hierarchy, the consequences of which are discussed below.

The influence of corporate patronage has always been felt in the governing bodies of the accountancy profession in so far as the public practitioner was oriented to the needs of business. The relative significance of corporate business for the practising accountant has grown in association with business amalgamations and the rise of the holding company: 'Thus the concentration of economic power brings with it a concentration of professional services. The concentration of audits, as a corollary, encourages the growth of large public practices at the expense of the small practitioner.'[1] Business amalgamation has encouraged the growth of large-scale public accountancy firms, whose senior partners dominated the executive councils of the associations, and

[1] Stacey, *English Accountancy*, p. 219.

which catered for the needs of powerful, corporative clients. Already by 1929 the expansion of these international firms had gone so far that 44 per cent of all public company audits in Britain were in the hands of thirty-nine firms, while in the United States 80 per cent of the American corporations listed by the Securities Exchange Commission were audited by six Anglo-American firms. Early in the century the London Association of Accountants complained that the spectacle of 'gigantic combines of accountants with branch offices all over the country and abroad [was] just as incongruous and inconsistent as would be that of large multiple firms of doctors or barristers'.[1]

Patronage, where it is the rule, creates the 'housed' practitioner. The aristocratic patron 'keeps' his artist, architect, doctor and priest; he maintains them on his estates or in some location socially or politically controlled by him. The practitioner is a courtier and must share the social manners and social graces of the courtier. Similarly, corporate patronage gives rise to the 'house' man, either directly as an employee or within the organisational context of a professional bureaucracy. These bureaucracies are large 'professional' firms and organisations which are dependent upon corporate business.

Patronage is associated with a fragmented, hierarchical, locally oriented occupational group. The 'housed' practitioner defers and refers to his patron or patrons and identifies with the court or the corporation, not primarily with the 'professional' community. In short, the evaluation of occupational role-performance is to a large extent in the hands of the patron. Fragmentation arises in response to the local needs of patrons; local knowledge and skills relevant to local demands are developed. Local reputation is an important basis of prestige and may depend more upon conformity with local customs and beliefs concerning non-professional matters than conformity with professionally defined norms. Institutionalised mechanisms again operate to maintain localism. Institutional contexts creating the conditions of peer-group solidarity and colleague community are less important. As Fromm pointed out, personal identity takes on an exchange value as all are dependent for their material success on a personal acceptance by those who need services and employ them.[2] Also, 'profes-

[1] *Certified Accountants Journal*, xxi (1929) 210.
[2] See E. Fromm, *The Sane Society* (London, 1956).

sional' practice is not a continuous and terminal career shared by all. Rather, in oligarchic forms the practitioner seeks 'preferment' which in the most successful cases leads to 'landed leisure', while the corporate practitioner can look forward to 'plum jobs' on boards of directors. Even the public accountant may have the ambition of moving into corporate management or may spend most of his time serving on boards of directors. As the employed accountant is promoted within the corporation in accordance with local criteria, so a 'professional' firm moves up the prestige hierarchy according to the size and influence of its patrons; the more big accounts it attracts, the higher its prestige. Community jargon is inhibited by the need to communicate with 'locals', while the authority of the patron reduces the clear function of ethics and autonomous disciplinary procedures. In the oligarchic case, standards are those of a consumption-oriented leisure class. The great physicians of the eighteenth century were known for their poetry, wit and elegance rather than being significantly evaluated by their colleagues in terms of technical competence. Occupationally defined norms have under corporate patronage less significance than corporately defined expectations. Thus the scope of ethics is narrowed by a relative increase in the number of salaried practitioners who serve a single client.

Finally, the homogeneous community which is characteristic of *professionalism* is displaced by hierarchical forms of occupational practice and organisation. The architect and physician under oligarchic patronage share, to a limited extent, the social position of their patrons. They rise in an occupational hierarchy through their association with more and more powerful patrons. Their prestige is social rather than narrowly and technically defined. The corporation hierarchy also provides positions of more or less status for incumbents, while the 'professional' bureaucracies are headed by managing partners or owners, men whose authority is defined by their position at the head of an organisational hierarchy.

The hierarchical fragmentation of the occupation may even be systematically expressed and institutionalised as dual systems of practice within a single occupation. The existence of an elite monopolising occupational service in a traditional context does not, of course, eliminate the needs of other social groups, which tend to be catered for by subordinate occupations and even in terms of divergent systems of knowledge. The hierarchy associated with corporate patronage may also be rationalised by the creation of subordinate technician grades of practitioner, allowing for greater specialisation and the sloughing-off of routine tasks by the occupation's leaders. Subordinate grades are generally effectively excluded from entrance to the higher grade. In engineering, accountancy and architecture in Britain this process has already been set in motion.

Patronage systems are characterised by practising contexts in which the practitioner must *know* and *do* what is expected of him. Consumer uncertainty is reduced at the expense of occupational autonomy. Under these conditions, knowledge tends to be local and basic research associated with the application of knowledge limited. These effects of patronage may be illustrated by the opposition of the accountancy profession to full public disclosure of company audits on the grounds that, while such disclosure might protect the shareholding public, it would imperil the competitive position of business firms. It has been claimed that the degree of independence which can be enjoyed by an accountant in preparing audit reports for public scrutiny is severely limited where his livelihood is effectively in the hands of those he is investigating in the public interest. Smaller firms of auditors, it was claimed by *The Economist* in 1932, 'may not always, in the present state of the law, be able to carry zeal for informative accounts to a logical end, in the face of opposition from a board effectively holding the power of the purse . . .'.[1]

This dependence on the business corporation has helped to create the pressure towards localism. The pursuit of basic knowledge is stressed less than knowledge specifically related to the needs of the patron. For example, the public nature of science develops where colleague evaluations are of major significance. The need to advance the competitive position of a corporate business patron reduces the significance of research communication which is geared to colleague evaluation, and research communication may be inhibited entirely where secrecy is an important element in competitive advantage. The body of theory applied by practitioners may also be affected by the demands of patronage. A major criterion of theory will be its applicability to

[1] Quoted by Stacey, *English Accountancy*, p. 185.

patron needs. As previously stated, in the context of such relationships consumer uncertainty is reduced at the expense of occupational autonomy. Knowledge tends to be particularistic in content and local in orientation. Accountancy, for example, has only in recent years developed at university level in Britain, but even so an increasing number of accountants receive their training within large, corporate businesses. Accountants' associations themselves have been marked by an apathetic attitude towards the development of basic accountancy knowledge through research. One commentator has gone so far as to claim that 'Among the vocations brought into prominence by the industrial revolution, accountancy was the only one whose growth and stature was for the most part unaccompanied by sustained research, either by its members or its professional organisations'.[1]

Particularism in the development of knowledge has been recognised as a major problem for the development of a unified accountancy occupation in so far as procedures, ground rules, techniques, continue to vary :

> The evolution of accountancy techniques has been severely practical. . . . Individual accountants in the course of their duty, especially when employed in industry, trade and commerce, frequently come across problems peculiar to their particular branch of endeavour and apply their basic training to solve special problems. . . . It is rarely . . . that any one particular system or the variation of a system is adopted by various firms facing the same problem, as each and every progenitor of a new method or technique in accounting prefers to utilise his own particular brain child.[2]

This tendency is not a product of the accountant's peculiar individualism as a personality, but stems from an orientation to local problems deriving from a system of control of the occupation which is fundamentally patron-based. Localism also introduces an ethic of limited responsibility, contrasting with that of *professionalism* – a situation in which the 'professional' does not look beyond the consequences of his actions for the patron. Also, such

[1] Ibid., p. 219.
[2] Ibid., p. 208.

practitioners tend to be apolitical, where the expression of political views or political action may embarrass the patron. Only recently in the field of engineering has the ethic of limited responsibility suffered a blow, and this is as a result of the increasing public concern about the consequences of environmental pollution. In response to a flood of criticism, engineers are just now beginning to discuss the general consequences of their actions which have in the past been geared to the needs of specific patrons. An important point here is that social problems of this kind may lead to the intervention of the state in attempting to control occupational practice. The consequences of such a move are discussed in the following section.

The neglect of research by patron-controlled occupations has also been associated with a slow development of formal education. Correspondence courses as the basic form of education for the British accountancy profession have survived because of the great stress laid upon local experience. This is not to say that 'articles', which are characteristic of professionalism rather than patronage, have not been significant in accountancy education. However, professionalism tends to be associated with the development of professionally controlled schools such as the Inns of Court.

Theoretical knowledge is, then, less important than knowledge which is applicable to the current practical needs of the patron. Practitioners are more likely to stress monist explanations which can be simply and immediately applied in policy or therapy. A stress on knowledge of this kind protects the practitioner in his need to *know* and *do*. Thus, medicine in the period of oligarchic patronage in England stressed monistic explanations of all disease, and blood-letting was a simple derived therapy. Developments in architectural knowledge have also responded to the needs of corporate patronage. System design which allows for variations in structure within certain limits laid down by the basic system is related to the fairly uniform needs of a single corporate patron with large-scale construction needs. The 'one-off' design related to the specific needs of a single 'client' is declining in importance as part of the architect's work.

The ideology of patronage systems stresses superior rather than equal competence within the occupation. Corporate practitioners are likely to express the view 'that some are more equal than others' in the attempt to justify the hierarchical organisation of the occupation, institutionalising this judgement by creating graded qualifications. Exclusiveness in the oligarchic system is, it has been argued above, related to the social hierarchy and the exclusion of those catering for the 'lower orders'. The hierarchy is also expressed in the ideas which justify the importance of the 'super' expert rather than the equal competence of all. Special knowledge and special experience become more important in defining the source of 'real' expertise. Such ideology may be stressed in struggles between corporation practitioners and general practitioners – who tend to stress ideologies of *professionalism*. This form of ideological struggle was clearly expressed in the battle between the physician elite and the apothecaries in eighteenth-century England.

The major tensions existing in patronage systems of occupational control are those produced by hierarchical organisation and dualistic systems of practice. Carr-Saunders and Wilson describe such a system as that operating at the beginning of the nineteenth century, when

> The medical profession was organised in a hierarchy with the physicians at the top and below, in descending order of prestige, 'the three inferior grades of surgeons, apothecaries and even druggists'. This form of organisation was not dictated by . . . the nature of medical technique. On the contrary it militated against the full employment of medical knowledge of the time. (1933, p. 75)

While dualism is a product of exclusivity and hierarchical organisation related to the needs of patronage, it also introduces areas of conflict and potential competition. The technician grades which are at present emerging in the British accountancy profession are likely to prove a potential source of tension as the interests of graduate and non-graduate grades diverge, just as the tensions between physicians and apothecaries shattered the organisation of the medical profession in the nineteenth century.

There are pressures towards elitism and localism as expressed in elitist cultural orientations and patron needs. The central tendency towards patronage in the development of accountancy in Britain has been subject to modifying forces. The accountants were creatures of *laissez-faire* capitalism which created a situation

73

in which the accountant was truly subservient to business interests. At the same time, however, those experiences of financial disaster associated with early forms of capitalism and pre-Keynesian economics, while stimulating the introduction of mechanisms of financial control within industry, also brought public clamour for some form of external control of the financing of public companies, leading to the introduction of various forms of public control, of accounting to the risk-bearer not only in the form of the investor but to the community at large. Also, as the role of the state became even more significant, not only in the control of production but also of consumption through such means as taxation, the elements of the accountant's role diversified even further. The accountants could not lose. The prop of capitalism, they became in the era of the planned economy a functional alternative to market forces. The significance of these changes is not only to be found in the direct employment of accountants by government and private corporations, but in the degree to which their functions have been hedged about by legislation. It is to the role of the state in mediating the producer–consumer relationship that we now turn.

6. MEDIATION

Various forms of mediative control of occupational activities are possible, but for present purposes we shall concentrate upon the conditions and characteristics of state control; that is, where the state intervenes in the relationship between practitioner and client in order to define needs and/or the manner in which such needs are catered for. It is important here to distinguish between the corporate patronage of public agencies and the mediative role of the state. Mediation arises where the state attempts to remove from the producer or the consumer the authority to determine the content and subjects of practice. It may do so with a minimum of encroachment upon an existing system of *professionalism*, through grants-in-aid to needy members of the public – grants which may be administered by the occupation itself. Where this is the case, the effect of intervention may be to support for a time at least existing institutions of *professionalism*. Legal aid, in many instances, operates in this way, by supporting underemployed practitioners who might otherwise be a source of dissension within the occupation, and a threat to the maintenance of the 'community'. At the other extreme, the state may attempt to ensure a desired distribution of occupational services through the medium of a state agency which is the effective employer of all practitioners who have a statutory obligation to provide a given service. This is the case with local government social services such as child welfare, health visiting, etc. The attempt to define who is to receive the service through the creation of a government agency will also give rise to supervision of the manner in which the service is provided – in Britain through such formal agencies as local government welfare committees or the school inspectorate. The influence of the state in Britain today may be gauged not only in terms of the state provision of various services, but also in the degree to which there exist legislative definitions of who may practise and under what conditions they may command the acquiescence of consumers.

The effect of state mediation has been to extend services to consumers who are defined on the basis of 'citizenship' rather than social origin or ability to pay fees. As a result there is an even greater diversity in the status characteristics of the consumers than is the case under *professionalism* and certainly under systems of *patronage*. However, the major significance of this form of control lies not in the social composition of the consumers but in the creation of a guaranteed 'clientele'. While it is generally agreed that state mediation in the provision of services associated with personal and social welfare operates to guarantee a service to everyone, its significance for the organisation and practice of an occupation rests largely in guaranteeing consumers. One consequence of the guarantee is that the referral system which is so important under *professionalism* in ensuring continuous colleague contact is less important where state mediation is the rule. The clients of probation officers are guaranteed by the workings of the system of justice, and referrals are less a matter of intra-occupational contacts than inter-occupational liaison with other social workers and medical men and the police. Aspects of uncertainty in the producer–consumer relationship are 'managed' by reducing possibilities of exploitation in both directions. The guarantee operates not only to increase the level of consumer demand,[1] but also reduces the practitioner's dependence upon 'clients' by limiting the consequences of consumer choice. The social character of the consumers is perhaps less important than their unique availability.

The state may also act in order to ensure a flow of services which are recognised as 'in the public good'. Rather than guaranteeing services to individuals, agencies are created in which engineers, for example, may work on problems of science application which have direct or indirect significance for the services provided by their practising colleagues. Such agencies may, however, directly service the needs of the state. In this case the consumer *is* the state and the agency is a product of patronage rather than state mediation between practitioner and 'client'.

It is clear from what has been said that under state mediation there is a diffusion of the consumer role itself. At times it becomes

[1] Many of the criticisms of the workings of the British National Health Service have been directed at the alleged over-use of medical services, particularly patient pressure on the general practitioner. It has been claimed that free access to the doctor has led to surgeries being crowded out by people with trivial complaints.

less apparent who the consumer is, and the clear-cut ethical prescriptions of *professionalism* which specify 'client' and colleague relationships are no longer entirely applicable. Again, the probation officer, as an officer of the courts, may find it difficult to determine his priorities and 'professional' responsibilities to the courts on the one hand and his probationers on the other.

State mediation will also tend to undermine existing social bases of recruitment. The control of recruitment to an occupation is an important means open to the state of ensuring that a universal service is provided, and it can achieve this end by expanding academic channels into the occupation. As a result, various forms of sponsorship and mechanisms of exclusiveness, such as the payment of fees to enter articles, are undermined. While under *professionalism* entry to an occupation is regulated by professionally controlled schools and examinations, state mediation has the effect of placing greater power in the hands of academic institutions such as universities and technical colleges. While it may be that these institutions are themselves staffed by members of the occupation, the shift in emphasis has the effect of changing the distribution of power within the 'community' at the expense of the practising membership. It has been argued by Dahrendorf that in Germany, for example, the relative power and prestige of academic lawyers has been associated with the degree to which the state has defined and controlled the career structure of law.[1]

Under state mediation various occupations are increasingly incorporated within the organisational framework of government agencies; solo practice is no longer the norm and the fiduciary relationship with clients is either modified or eliminated. The income of practitioners may be in the form of salaries or determined in accordance with a system of payment geared to the level and amount of services provided on the basis of per capita or unit payments. Also, elements of the bureaucratic role become interwoven with the occupational role in service organisations, the result being a general dilemma stemming from the problem of balancing administrative and consumer needs.[2] As in the system of

[1] R. Dahrendorf, 'The Education of an Elite: Law Faculties and the German Upper Class', *Transactions of the Fifth World Congress of Sociology*, III (Louvain, 1964) 259–74.

[2] For a discussion of this 'dilemma', see P. Blau and W. R. Scott, *Formal Organisations: A Comparative Approach* (London, 1963).

corporate patronage, the bureaucratisation of the occupation tends to stratify practitioners and formalise incipient cleavages. Such differentiation may destroy colleague relationships and neutralise the controls which an autonomous profession imposes on its members.[1]

State mediation has, then, the effect of creating divergent interests and orientations within an occupational community as a result of the creation of varied specialist and hierarchical organisational forms. These divisions threaten the maintenance or inhibit the emergence of the 'complete community' of *professionalism* and even the belief in occupation-wide colleagueship, as was pointed out by Bucher and Strauss in describing occupations where a high degree of specialisation had developed: 'In so far as colleagueship refers to a relationship characterised by a high degree of shared interests and common symbols, it is probably rare that all members of a profession are even potentially colleagues' (1961, p. 330). Rather, they claim, specialisation gives rise to competing segments in loose amalgamation at best, pursuing varied interests and missions. The fact that occupational interests and ideologies are divergent also suggests that no dominant power group can emerge on the basis of occupational location alone. The creation of a technocracy of the kind which Veblen envisaged is unlikely where the conditions of state mediation prevail. Dualistic systems of practice are also a less likely consequence of hierarchical organisation where the attempt to guarantee services also implies the provision of 'equal service to all'. Rather, the result is an explosion in the numbers of generalist practitioners or the creation of separate but equal specialisms. In Britain, social work has developed within the context of state agencies, and no single 'generalist' social work occupation has yet managed to impose a controlling diagnostic relationship on other specialist groups, although a number, including the psychiatric social workers, believe that it is their destiny to do so.

Not only is localism (discussed above in Section 5) a possible consequence of state mediation where, for example, practitioners identify with the special conditions of a local government organi-

[1] The tensions which may arise in professionally manned bureaucracies are identified by W. R. Scott, 'Professionals in Bureaucracies: Areas of Conflict', in Vollmer and Mills (1966, pp. 264–75).

sation, but divergent and sometimes opposed interests are generated between those in managerial and non-managerial positions, between one agency and another, and between the 'centre' and the 'periphery', that is, between the administration and the field workers within a given service. Differences in the structural or organisational location of practitioners are, then, likely to generate divergences of orientation; there will accordingly be varying *degrees* of self-identification with the occupational community. We may find that the simultaneous existence of organisational and occupational affiliations affects the extent to which individuals become committed to administrative needs or the problem of 'client' groups. A 'client' orientation is likely to be characteristic of practitioners close to the 'periphery' whose relationships with their 'clients' are more meaningful and immediate than those with their socially distant colleagues and superiors. In recent years there have been a number of cases, particularly in the United States, where the 'authorities' have complained that social welfare officers and field social workers have become 'overinvolved' in the plight of their charges, so much so that social workers have taken up leadership positions within the community to seek political solutions to their clients' problems.

Localism is likely to be expressed where practitioners are located in the administrative hierarchies of community agencies. This would be true in Britain of public health officers, chief nursing officers and municipal treasurers, among others, whose careers are entirely within local government service. However, practice within the occupation is not a continuous and terminal career, as service agencies provide access to managerial and administrative positions. Cosmopolitanism (which may involve identification with the occupational community or a wider community such as that of all scientists or all educators) is more likely to be the product of academic and research-centred locations. The *patronage* and state mediation of science helps to explain a seeming paradox – that the growth of scientific expertise, while increasing the prestige and legitimacy of science itself, has been associated with a decline in the power and prestige of individual scientists.

Under this form of institutionalised control the functions of occupational associations in maintaining colleague identification (by the means described above in Section 4) are likely to be less important than are its specifically 'trade union functions' in pressing for improvements in pay and conditions. The functions of bestowing status and identity are sometimes shared with agencies other than the occupational association or are completely taken over by agencies such as the employing bureaucracy. Negotiations for improved income and conditions are carried out by a single occupational association or, perhaps, by a parallel organisation specifically set up for bargaining purposes in order not to compromise the 'professional' stance of the association. Where the functions of maintaining standards are taken over by state agencies, or are provided for in legislation, the association is transformed into an occupational pressure group, effectively losing its powers to prescribe the manner of practice. The degree to which trade union functions do become dominant will depend on the degree to which the state is involved in determining the manner in which occupational services are to be carried out. Where a colleague system, symbolised by the association, still largely controls the content of practice, as is the case with medicine in Britain today, the ethical and community functions of the association remain important. The various branches of social work on the other hand enjoy little autonomy in determining the content of practice, and social work ethics are largely encompassed in the rules of the agencies which employ them. As with *patronage*, it is unlikely that the general practitioners will play the most significant role in occupational associations. Hughes has argued, for example, that 'the professional conscience . . . will be lodged in that segment of professionals who work in complicated settings, for they must, in order to survive, be sensitive to more problems and a greater variety of points of view'.[1]

Variations in the organisational and structural locations of practitioners will not only lead to differences in attitudes regarding the occupational community, but also to differences in the types of knowledge and ideologies espoused. It is often claimed that the intervention of the state into various areas of the 'knowledge industry' has led in recent years to an over-concentration on applied research at the expense of basic research. This view is, in part, a result of confusing the consequences of *patronage* and *mediative* forms of control. The pressures towards applied re-

[1] E. C. Hughes, 'Professions', in *Daedalus* (1963, p. 666).

search are strong in a system of *patronage*, where the needs of the consumer are paramount (as is the case with scientists employed by governments in relation to defence needs). State mediation, however, by guaranteeing consumers and creating bureaucratic organisational contexts where dependence upon them is even further reduced, can lead, as Ben-David has argued, to greater research orientation.[1] The organisation man may pick his problems if not his clients. Where there are competing norms of 'science' and 'service', as Ben-David calls them, state mediation of the practitioner–client relationship provides a wide variety of organisational contexts within which a science orientation is more likely to be sustained. This appears to undermine the conventional view that bureaucracy in all its forms stultifies innovation. However, a distinction must also be drawn between structural conditions conducive to research and the generation of new ideas and conditions conducive to the implementation of innovatory ideas.

The occupational community as a whole is, under mediative control, no longer the repository of specialised knowledge. Where state mediation creates large-scale bureaucratic service agencies, it is likely that practising members of the occupation will no longer be the chief source of technical advance in the field, as in the case under *professionalism*. The practitioner loses initiative in the development of knowledge to full-time research institutions. The mediative role of the state may also lead to technical and ethical questions being removed from the occupation's control. Even in medicine, questions of drug control leading to legislative definitions of medical responsibility, or official discussions of the ethics of heart-transplant surgery, have intruded upon previously accepted boundaries of occupational responsibility. The extension of such problems to the public sphere led in 1970 to the complaint that it was unsatisfactory that 'such decisions were being made by politicians, advised by civil servants, with the doctor kept at arm's length'.[2]

[1] J. Ben-David, 'The Professional Role of the Physician in Bureaucratised Medicine: A Study in Role Conflict', *Human Relations*, XI 3 (Aug 1958) 255–74.

[2] Report of an address to the British Association by Dr Henry Miller, *The Times*, 9 Sep 1970.

83

One of the major ideological orientations accompanying state mediation is a stress on social service – on the broad social consequences of the provision of services in general rather than upon the personal service orientation of *professionalism*. As vocational education, research and resources are more and more supplied or affected by state actions, various occupations find themselves increasingly anticipating, responding to, and seeking to control such actions. In so doing they are forced to relate their policies to the social and political consequences of their actions. Consideration of social welfare, social and preventative medicine, law reform, etc., will bring practitioners more explicitly into the political arena. This is not to suggest that they are more likely to be involved in politics as parliamentary and local government candidates or political commentators, but that their political involvement will stem directly from their occupational interests rather than from their views as citizens. The 'authoritative' pronouncement common under a system of *professionalism* gives way to the incorporation of practitioners, as advisers and experts, within the context of government decision-making.

It has been argued that where the area of expertise enjoyed by an occupation shrinks as a result of bureaucratisation of tasks, the practitioner will seek to expand the range of his authority by accepting advisory and managerial positions.[1] Where an occupation extends its authority through 'non-professional' means, purely 'professional' sources of authority and the 'community' aspect of the occupation are undermined. Also, where an occupation attempts to maintain inviolate a community of monopolised skills even though the basis of practice is changing, it is likely to lose practice to others. For example, the attempt to maintain the traditional organisation of law in Britain during a period of state expansion has led to the rise of the quasi-judicial administrative tribunals – two thousand of which function in Britain today – as an alternative to the courts. Under state mediation, efficiency becomes a major yardstick in determining whether one form of organisation or another is superior in terms of its social welfare function. There is no generally accepted belief that the independent solo practitioner necessarily provides the 'best' foundation for the organisation of practice. There will still be attempts to

[1] This point is made by King (1968, pp. 44–5).

justify existing or increased rewards in terms of the social value of the service, but it is recognised that the value can be increased by greater efficiency.

A system of control which allows for a variety of organisational forms is bound to generate a number of tensions. Many of the tensions created by state mediation are characteristic of bureaucratic forms as such. There is, however, a central dilemma which is a conflict between the demands of service and administrative needs. The attempt to guarantee services gives rise to an administrative framework, the efficient operation of which creates demands which are in conflict with the provision of those services for which they were created. The growth of bureaucratic structures geared to the provision of services has given rise to what Kornhauser refers to as pluralist bureaucracies,[1] where occupational career structures and rewards systems are differentiated out from the administrative hierarchy in order to accommodate occupational expectations. The recent reorganisation of local authority social services in England provides an example of restructuring the bureaucracy in order to provide a career line leading to the administrative position of Director of Social Services, so accommodating the career aspirations of social workers within a bureaucratic setting.

Bureaucratisation is a major underlying process associated with mediative control resulting, in part, from the attempt to guarantee services and consumers. The general scheme suggests that we might distinguish various ways in which 'professionals' become bureaucratised: (a) as a consequence of corporate patronage, through the creation of occupationally-owned and managed bureaucracies; (b) as a second consequence of corporate patronage, through the direct employment of practitioners as 'house' men; (c) as a consequence of state mediation, through the creation of state-controlled service agencies. In sociological literature, the 'bureaucratisation of professionals' is generally seen as an undifferentiated process with uniform consequences for occupational organisation, practice and orientation. It is now suggested that each type presented has varying consequences for occupational practice and is the product of different institutionalised forms of control.

[1] Kornhauser, *Scientists in Industry.* *(see p. 11, n. 1)*

It is clear that state mediation as a form of control leads to great differentiation in the organisation and practice of a variety of occupations. The proliferation of organisational contexts is in itself an important feature of the form of control. Nevertheless, the consequence of state intervention in the producer–consumer relationship in guaranteeing a 'clientele' introduces a major distinction between mediative forms of control and the other types discussed.

7. CONCLUSION

The problems posed by the crystallisation and emergence of new occupations and the institutionalised orders which arise to control them are numerous. This study has been an attempt to work within the existing conventions in the field of the 'sociology of professions' while, at the same time, suggesting new departures in the framing of the problems. It has been argued that if we can successfully extricate ourselves from the strait-jacket of conceptualising all problems in terms of the unilineal concept of professionalisation, we shall have opened up the discussion and laid the ground for a more fruitful analysis of a wide variety of problems in the sociology of occupations.

The conditions which gave rise to the institutions of professionalism are no longer dominant in industrialised societies – a fact which should direct attention to alternative forms of control such as those suggested in the discussion of patronage and mediative systems. Nor will these alternative institutions of control be relevant only for an analysis of those occupations conventionally regarded as professions and associated with a 'gentlemanly' image. It has already been mentioned above that the significance of consumer durables for the 'good life' as defined in a mass-consumption economy has given rise to acute problems of control in areas of occupational practice related to 'servicing' rather than 'service', and traditionally unrelated to the 'professions' as such. It is possible to speculate about the consequences of these developments for the growing strength of consumer movements and the emergence of 'communalism' as a form of 'client' control. The recognition that alternative forms of occupational control are possible also sensitises us to possibilities of analysing the emergence of occupations in developing societies where forms of patronage and mediation are likely to be more significant than professionalism. Any attempt to apply measures of professionalisation to emergent occupations in Africa and Asia is as a result highly likely to prove abortive and would ultimately be a trivialisation of the problem. It is hoped, then, that the typology presented here would make possible fruitful comparative studies not only of different occupations, but of culturally distinct locations of occupational development.

The claim that occupational organisation and practice are to be understood only in terms of the prevailing type of control to which an occupation is subjected also brings into sharper focus questions relating to the power resources available to occupational groups as well as other social groupings who may attempt to supervise the application of knowledge and skills to further their own or others' interests. This emphasis brings us back full circle to a consideration of those problems which exercised earlier sociologists and social commentators – that of evaluating the role of the 'professions' in society. However, rather than viewing all such occupations as undifferentiated in their consequences, we may expect that practitioners subject to corporate patronage, for example, will exhibit beliefs, attitudes and ideologies which diverge from and sometimes conflict with those exhibited by practitioners subjected to mediative or collegiate forms of control.

Finally, the purpose of this study and the typology presented has been to suggest that while the major themes which informed the beginnings of the 'sociology of professions' asked questions and suggested answers which focused upon the relationship of the professions to other power groupings in society, the major approaches associated with 'trait' theory and functionalism which adopt 'professionalisation' as the core concept of this discipline fail to address such problems in a meaningful way. The basis of this failure has been the acceptance of a model of professions which cannot account for variations in the institutional frame work of professional practice. The typology presented attempts to outline such a framework. It does so by focusing upon the client–professional relationship, stressing not only variations in the potentiality for autonomy of an occupation, but also variations in the social characteristics of the consumer as a fundamental condition giving rise to variations in institutionalised forms of control. It is hoped that the refinement of such an approach will re-create interest in those themes discussed in the introduction and suggest answers to the seeming paradox which distinguishes assessments of the role of the professions in society, indicating that this paradox is a product of the concentration on distinct areas of occupational life and even different occupations which are not uniform in character and development, but are a product of variant institutionalised forms of occupational control.

BIBLIOGRAPHY

M. Abrahamson, *The Professional in the Organisation* (Chicago, 1967). A collection of readings bringing together material on a wide range of professionals working in large-scale organisations.

J. Ben-David, 'Professions in the Class System of Present Day Societies', *Current Sociology*, xii 3 (1963–4). An attempt to revitalise the questions about the place of the professions in the class systems of different societies, mainly through a discussion of the way in which professionalisation is reflected in the development of higher education in various societies, so affecting levels of social mobility.

R. Bucher and A. Strauss, 'Professions in Process', *American Journal of Sociology*, lxvi (Jan 1961) 325–34. A critique of the 'community' approach to professions which focuses on diversity and conflict of interest giving rise to 'cliques' and 'missions' within a profession; the implication of these processes for change.

A. M. Carr-Saunders and P. A. Wilson, *The Professions* (Oxford, 1933; reprinted by Frank Cass, 1964). A seminal work in the sociology of professions which has not been surpassed in the forty years since its publication. It deals with the historical development and modern organisation of a large number of professional groups including lawyers, doctors, dentists, nurses, veterinary surgeons, engineers, chemists, physicists, architects, surveyors, accountants and teachers. Apart from the historical survey of professional bodies, it is still of analytical worth and its insights still stimulate much of the thinking in the field today.

'The Professions', *Daedalus* (fall 1963). A special issue of the journal of the American Academy of Arts and Sciences, devoted to the professions, with important general essays by Bernard Barber and Everett C. Hughes. Other articles are devoted to the legal and medical professions in the United States as well as the clergy, teachers, scientists, the military, psychiatry, city planners and politicians.

A. Etzioni, *The Semi-Professions and their Organisation: Teachers, Nurses, and Social Workers* (New York, 1969). A collection of essays on teachers, nurses and social workers which attempts to apply the notion of the semi-professions to these occupations as a means of distinguishing them from fully professionalised occupations.

W. J. Goode, 'Community within a Community: The Professions', *American Sociological Review*, xxii (Apr 1957) 194–200. The professions as communities in which colleagues share a sense of identity, values, a continuing status and common language. A discussion of how these community aspects of occupations are maintained and what strains they are subject to.

P. Halmos, *The Personal Service Society* (London, 1970). An attempt to evaluate the social significance of the professions, arguing that the ideology of the 'personal service professions' has seeped into general belief systems and is becoming the dominant ideology in industrial societies, whatever their political complexion.

E. C. Hughes, *Men and their Work* (Glencoe, Ill., 1958). Essays on the social-psychological aspects of work, professionals and professional aspirants.

J. A. Jackson (ed.), *Professions and Professionalisation* (Cambridge, 1970). A collection of essays presenting a variety of 'new' approaches to the study of professions.

M. D. King, 'Science and the Professional Dilemma', in Julius Gould (ed.), *Penguin Social Sciences Survey, 1968* (Harmondsworth, 1968). A 'crisis' in the professions is identified as arising from attempts to balance the demands of status enhancement on the one hand and occupational identity on the other. The general theme is illustrated by developments in science.

D. S. Lees, *The Economic Consequences of the Professions* (Institute of Economic Affairs, London, 1966). An economist's case for reducing restrictive practices in the British professions.

R. Lewis and A. Maude, *Professional People* (London, 1952). The development of the professions in Britain, showing particular concern for the way in which the 'intervention' of the state into professional practice has undermined the independence of professional people to the detriment of social life in general and democracy in particular.

T. H. Marshall, 'The Recent History of Professionalism in Relation to Social Structure and Social Policy', *Canadian Journal of Economic and Political Science* (Aug 1939), reprinted in *Sociology at the Crossroads and Other Essays* (London, 1963). An essay on the nature of professionalism, taking as central the service ethic. The effect of developments in social welfare policies on professionals' service orientations.

G. Millerson, *The Qualifying Associations: A Study in Professionalisation* (London, 1964). A study of the significance of the qualifying associations in the development of professional occupations in Britain; their organisation, functions in the provision of education, control over professional conduct.

Monopolies Commission, *Report on Professional Services*, 2 vols, Cmnd 4463–4 (H.M.S.O., London, 1970). 'A report on the general effect on the public interest of certain restrictive practices so far as they prevail in relation to the supply of professional services.'

T. Parsons, 'The Professions and Social Structure', in *Essays in Sociological Theory*, rev. ed. (Glencoe, Ill., 1954) pp. 34–49. A comparison of business and the professions, arguing for their structural similarity in industrial societies, yet making the distinction between the collectivity-orientation of the professions as against the self-orientation of the business community.

W. J. Reader, *Professional Men* (London, 1966). A history of the development of the professions in nineteenth-century England. The establishment of the major professional associations and the struggles and reforms leading to their enhanced status by the end of the century.

D. Rueschemeyer, 'Doctors and Lawyers: A Comment on the Theory of the Professions', *Canadian Review of Sociology and Anthropology*, I (Feb 1964) 17–30. A critique of the functionalist theory of the professions which examines law and medicine in the light of general functionalist assumptions about the relevance of professional practice to 'central social values' and the homogeneity of the professions.

H. L. Smith, 'Contingencies of Professional Differentiation', *American Journal of Sociology*, LXIII (Jan 1958) 410–14. Some conditions and consequences of specialisation and fission within professional 'communities'.

H. M. Vollmer and D. L. Mills, *Professionalisation* (Englewood

Cliffs, N.J., 1966). A wide selection of readings relating to such subjects as the concept of professionalisation, the social context of professionalisation, professional associations and colleague relations, professionals in complex organisations, professionals and government, etc.

H. Wilensky, 'The Professionalisation of Everyone?', *American Journal of Sociology*, LXIX (Sep 1964). A paper rejecting the view that many occupations are in process of 'professionalising', that deviations in the process by which the newer so-called professional occupations have emerged suggest also the emergence of different structural forms. Very few occupations will achieve the authority of the established professions.